learn to ·
swim

ROB & KATHY McKAY

learn to •
swim

Step-by-step water confidence and safety
skills for babies and young children

A DORLING KINDERSLEY BOOK

LONDON, NEW YORK, MUNICH, MELBOURNE, DELHI

Senior editor Salima Hirani
Senior art editor Hannah Moore
Project editor Claire Wedderburn-Maxwell
Project art editor Tracy Timson
DTP designer Julian Dams
Production controller Shwe Zin Win
Managing editor Liz Coghill
Managing art editors Glenda Fisher, Emma Forge
Art director Carole Ash
Publishing manager Anna Davidson
Publishing director Corinne Roberts

First published in Great Britain in 2005
by Dorling Kindersley Limited
80 Strand, London WC2R ORL
A Penguin company

A CIP catalogue record for this book is available from the British Library.

Neither the authors nor the publisher can be held responsible for any
damage or injury resulting from baby swimming.

ISBN 1 4053 0323 9

Reproduced by Colourscan, Singapore
Printed and bound by Star Standard, Singapore

See our complete catalogue at **www.dk.com**

CONTENTS

INTRODUCTION

Learning to swim can be one of the most rewarding experiences of childhood. It is a celebration, a rite of passage and a gift of freedom. Reintroducing your baby to the water at a young age makes perfect sense — after all, your little swimmer was surrounded by water in the womb for nine months.

People around the world use water for relaxation, play, therapy, ritual, health, nourishment, invigoration and exercise. Water is an integral part of our human heritage, physical make-up and planet. In water we are weightless, free, caressed and cleansed. Babies can enter this unique natural element and its altered gravity in a non-stressful, harmonious manner. Your baby can learn to swim months before he can walk, and it will be easier for him to propel himself to you in the water, rather than learn to pull himself up, fight gravity and walk towards you. None of us remember learning to walk, and in much the same way a baby who learns to swim at an early age, as part of a gradual, child-centred approach, won't remember a time when he couldn't swim and claim water citizenship.

Who better to teach your baby to swim than the people he trusts the most? We believe parents are a baby's best teachers, on land and in the water, and have therefore adapted our established swim-school programme specifically for this book, so that we can pass on the wealth of knowledge we have gained from our nurturing and stimulating child-friendly classes. *Learn to Swim* is designed to help parents establish an optimal learning environment for children aged six months to four years. Utilizing our combined 50 years of experience in teaching thousands of babies and children to swim, we will guide you to successfully create a watery classroom full of positive reinforcement, colour, music, stimulation, laughter and motivation.

Our common-sense approach places your child at the centre of the learning. He will learn and develop swimming skills through games, songs, humour, praise and developmentally appropriate skill activities. You will follow a child-paced, step-by-step learning progression especially designed for very young swimmers. And although this book is for parents who are teaching their own children to swim, we hope swimming teachers will also find it useful and integrate our gentle approach to baby swimming into their programmes.

Learning is a process, not a product — it should occur at the child's pace, when he is open, receptive, relaxed and ready. We teach swimming — not thrashing — and that takes patience, practice and a great deal of time, and when you give your child that time and patience, you lay a foundation of mutual respect and trust that you can build on in other areas of your lives. Teaching your child to swim in this supportive and caring way is not just about helping him to learn water confidence and safety skills. It is also about you developing a teaching style in relation to the way your child learns, encouraging and supporting him rather than being demanding and demeaning, and replacing the pressure to learn with the desire to learn.

Celebrate each small step along the way, and remember that there is no need to rush or force your child to perform as there will be periods of skill assimilation and learning plateaus. Read your baby's body language and assess his level of readiness to determine the course of each lesson. We want your child to enjoy this experience from his very first trip to the pool, in the hope that he will continue to enjoy swimming for a lifetime. As you play with your baby in the pool, you are not only teaching movement through the water, but fostering exploration, curiosity, trust, joy, wonder, risk-taking, confidence, grace and endurance.

In the first chapter of the book, we introduce all the essential basics: the philosophy of our teaching; the many benefits of baby swimming; what you need to take to the pool; positive, child-friendly teaching methods; and comprehensive water safety strategies. The second chapter, Water Confidence, is divided into stages that are based on age. In this chapter, we take you through the initial phases of water adjustment, how to teach your child to hold his breath for submersion, then onwards towards the exciting moment when your baby takes his first swim between two people. Once your baby can comfortably perform all the age-appropriate skills in this section, you will move on to the intermediate swimming skills, such as turning around under water, floating and diving for rings, as shown in the third chapter, Swimming Unaided.

We hope this family experience is a remarkable one for both you and your child. Delight in the giggles and splashes, the time you have to bond in the pool and the excitement and pride your child shows as he develops new skills. So grab your swimsuits and let's go to the pool...

INTRODUCING BABY SWIMMING

Water, babies, laughter and learning to swim… it's an unbeatable combination. When approached in a nurturing, child-friendly way, baby swimming offers your child numerous benefits, including boundless joy and increased self-esteem and confidence. It enhances your baby's physical and personal development, resulting in a happy, healthy and well-adjusted child. Our journey begins with an important first step — an informed parent. The goal of this chapter is to help you become a confident, active and trusted learning partner for your child.

THE BENEFITS OF BABY SWIMMING

There is a wide range of benefits available to babies and children who are taught to swim in a gentle, gradual, child-paced way. Researchers have documented some of the measurable positive effects of baby swimming and, around the world, parents have witnessed first-hand the many enhancements to mental, physical, emotional, developmental and social well-being that result from teaching their children to swim.

EMOTIONAL BENEFITS

Swimming allows babies to move independently much sooner than they are able to on dry land. Imagine the boost of confidence and self-esteem that movement through the water brings your child as she explores her new, watery environment. Every time you catch your child after a jump or a short swim, she learns trust. When you praise her for each small achievement on the way to mastering a skill, you build her self-esteem. Babies' faces glow after they accomplish a task successfully — they look for approval and validation, and parental acknowledgment of their efforts fosters their personal self-acceptance and pride. Swimming can be very empowering for babies, as it offers them a new sense of freedom.

Parent-child bonding

Where else but in the water can you commune face-to-face, skin-to-skin, with your baby for extended periods of time in a warm and inviting natural element? Teaching your baby to swim increases your bond with her as you play together and move in unison, exercising patience, encouragement and kindness towards her. You will learn about her growing personality, sense of humour and how she approaches new situations. As you teach her, you will become aware of her learning style and her changing needs and abilities. This knowledge will not only aid successful baby swimming but will also help you establish positive parenting methods that you can use outside the pool.

STUDIES INTO BABY SWIMMING

A study conducted by Professor Liselott Diem from 1974 to 1976 at the German Sports College in Cologne, found that children who learned to swim at an early age demonstrated advanced development in:

◎ motor skills

◎ reaction time (reflexes)

◎ power of concentration (focus)

◎ intelligence

◎ social behaviour

◎ social interaction

◎ self-confidence

◎ independence

◎ coping with new and unfamiliar situations.

Overall, children were found to be more well-adjusted than their peers who had not participated in early swimming programmes, and the increase in both self-esteem and independence due to baby swimming were cited as contributory factors. The study also concluded that children who swam from an early age benefited from positive interaction and bonding with their parent.

SOCIAL BENEFITS

If you can gather a group of like-minded parents and teach your children together, they will reap the social benefits — they learn from their peers by observing and mimicking them, and also enjoy their company. Children begin to look forward to interacting with each other, learning to take turns, to share and to try new skills.

PHYSICAL BENEFITS

All the benefits to fitness that swimming brings adults — an increase in strength, muscle tone, endurance and lung capacity — are also enjoyed by children. For young babies, movement through the water liberates them from a comparatively static life, and allows them to exercise muscles that would not yet be used. For older babies, swimming is the natural complement to their growing repertoire of land-based skills. Because both sides of the body are involved in swimming, and therefore both lobes of the brain, swimming increases coordination, motor development and balance. Parents also see better sleep patterns after swimming.

PERSONAL SAFETY

With time, practice and developmental capability, children can acquire the necessary swimming safety skills to aid them in the event of a water emergency. A calm child who feels at home in the water and who has regularly practised safety skills with her parent will not panic, but will rather proactively implement the techniques she has learned. Note, however, that no child should ever be considered "drownproof", and you should always be vigilant when your child is in the water.

POSITIVE TEACHING METHODS

Being a proactive, positive parent helps to nurture a well-adjusted, happy child. When teaching your baby to swim at such a young age, you have an opportunity to build trust, share joy, communicate by touch and words and bond with your child as he experiences new and varied stimuli. The impact you have on your child at this young age cannot be underestimated, and baby swimming is a unique opportunity to develop and put good teaching practices into action.

THE CHILD-CENTRED APPROACH

We live in an era that has benefited from research into the capabilities of babies. No longer seen simply as little lumps, babies regularly astound scientists with their innate abilities. We now know how even a very young baby can discern faces, language and emotion, and how activities and experiences affect his mental development.

Although babies develop many skills from an early age, parents should not attempt to create a "super baby". Children should not be pressurized or pushed to perform, but guided to develop their skills at a rate they are comfortable with.

PROGRESS AT YOUR CHILD'S PACE

Just as all children do not learn to walk, talk or read at the same age, nor do they learn to swim at the same rate. As a parent, it is critical that you do not place any accelerated expectations ahead of your child's actual readiness to learn a skill. All children learn to kick when they swim – but some do it on the first day, while others do it only after a great deal of time, motivation and practise. Kicking on the first day doesn't make one child better, smarter or stronger than another child who learns later – it simply means they are different and unique individuals.

Don't worry about how quickly your child learns a new technique, just focus on acquiring a skill a little bit at a time. Make the most of the process and the time you are spending together doing an activity you both enjoy, and remember the most important thing is to make your lessons fun and playful.

Comfort in the pool

Both children and parents bring with them a host of previous water experiences – some positive and some negative. Some babies have been in the bath or shower with water pouring over their face from just a few days old; others have seen their older brother or sister swim under water; while others are fearful of the water because of a water scare or a previous bad experience with an aggressive swimming programme. Some children are shy and want to assess a new situation from a distance; others show an inherent aversion to having water on their faces; while some children bolt immediately into a new environment without a care.

Remember also, if you are the gregarious parent of a reserved and cautious child, you will need to respect the fact that you have your own individual differences, and learn from your child what makes him secure, comfortable and happy in the pool.

THE IMPORTANCE OF BODY LANGUAGE

Even before your baby can speak, he is a very capable interpreter of your body language, and will pick up on the slightest nuances. Your facial expressions, muscle tension, tone of voice and reactions will all convey clues to your child about his environment and how he should act. It is therefore vital that you are relaxed and confident with him in the water, as he will pick up on your cues, whether positive or negative.

◎ A relaxed, gentle touch and upbeat, playful or calm tone conveys a sense of ease to your child.

◎ Use positive signals such as smiles, hugs, applause, laughter or a kiss to reassure your child and reinforce a positive atmosphere.

◎ Don't send mixed signals – for example, don't force your child to carry out a manoeuvre and then give him a hug or a kiss. Use encouragement rather than coercion.

You should watch and interpret your child's body language carefully – especially if he is too young to speak – as this will help you to assess his comfort level and whether he is happy with the skills or games that you are practising.

◎ A relaxed, happy, smiling child is enjoying the experience. Note that his muscle tension will feel soft, not tight or tense.

◎ If your child is clinging to you, it means that he is not ready and needs more time to adjust to a new situation. Don't rush him or pull him away from you, but give him the security he is seeking.

◎ Crying is your baby's way of telling you that something is wrong, and signals a need to stop what you are doing. Redirect your child's attention with a toy or by playing a different game, and assess what caused the crying.

FEAR VERSUS LOVE

Some parents and swimming programmes see water as the enemy — a lethal danger to be feared, and a threat to be dealt with. These "drownproofing" or "survival" swimming programmes often rely on aggressive methods, such as forced back floating. Skills are goal-oriented and must be acquired rapidly by the child in order for her to save herself if she enters the water unexpectedly. A parent is generally not present in the water during the lessons in case the child relies on her parent to help her.

These aggressive methods are in complete opposition to the child-centred approach, which is based on love of the child, love of water and love of learning. We believe that this positive focus — and the fun it fosters — leads to much more successful learning than a fearful environment can produce. Water is seen as a wonderful medium for growth and development, and the parent is always in the water, bonding with his or her child, facilitating learning and assisting with the gradual acquisition of skills. This means that the parent knows exactly what their child can and cannot do in the water, for how long she can hold her breath and how competent a swimmer she is. The parent also recognizes their own responsibility to safeguard their baby and to implement a comprehensive water safety strategy (see pp24–25).

COPING WITH CRANKINESS

Everybody is allowed a bad day occasionally, and sometimes children will have a bad five minutes or an entirely bad week. Often this crankiness may be unrelated to swimming — teething is a common problem, as is a missed or interrupted sleep, hunger or a change in routine (for example if one parent is away). It is important for you to be sensitive to the physical energy levels and mood of your child and to not push her.

Hopefully, just being in the water will help your child feel better. If you are swimming with other children, your child will benefit from observing everyone else swimming. Observation time for a child may mean she will try a skill later in the bath or on her next trip to the pool, mimicking what she saw earlier. Use these "off" days to focus on the skills that your child enjoys, relax the pace of your lesson and sing and play together.

YOUR ROLE IN THE POOL

Being in the water with your child is vital as it creates an immediate sense of security. A parent provides familiarity and can progress through the lesson at the child's pace. Is your child relaxed and ready to try something new, or is she tense, stressed or frightened and in need of more time to adjust? The parent's role is one of conscious and aware observer as well as instructor. How you present new material and skills to your child will be as important as the skills themselves. As this is a child-centred approach, always go at her pace, and remember that your tone of voice, mood and muscle tension send strong messages (see box, p13).

COMPARING TEACHING METHODS

Aggressive swimming programmes use pressure and coercion to achieve rigid goals. The child-centred approach is very different, and progresses at the child's pace.

GOAL-DOMINATED PROGRAMME	CHILD-CENTRED PROGRAMME
skill comes first	child comes first
time-frame is rigid, and there is pressure to perform	time-frame is flexible and depends on child's readiness
force and coercion are used to teach survival skills	gentle guiding and encouragement help a child accomplish goals
teacher is dominant	progress at child's pace
no-nonsense format	fun, playful learning

FOCUS ON THE MOMENT

Because your child's swimming lessons may be his first educational outing, they should be positive experiences that lead to many other educational successes as he grows up. It's up to you to get into your child's frame of mind: focus on the game, the adventure, the colour, the fun and the laughter. Remember that your child will be much more focused on the moment – on the simple delights and novel experiences – and shouldn't be rushed. Try to recall how thrilling your first ever trip to a swimming pool was and what your child must be excited by: the feel of water on his skin, the bright toys, the sight of water all around him and the other people in the pool.

MAKING SWIMMING LESSONS FUN

Crying is not a prerequisite for learning to swim, so never let an ill-informed relative or teacher tell you that this is the case. Add skills slowly when your child is ready, never pushing him beyond his abilities, and remember that forcing skills on children is contrary to every sound learning theory. Your own swimming programme should resemble all the best land-based programmes for the relevant age group and contain those elements that best suit early education – games, toys, fun and laughter.

Being patient

Make sure that you are relaxed and having fun during your swimming lessons, enjoying the giggles and splashes that naturally accompany learning. Be patient with your child if he hates jumping off the wall or putting his face in the water – he is bound to surprise you in the end. Don't let your tone of voice or your words betray you and indicate to your child your disappointment or frustration. Instead, try another tactic or switch to another skill. Often, simply time and exposure are required before a new skill seems less intimidating and begins to look like fun and worth trying.

Using humour

Somehow, silliness has become the universal unspoken language that all children understand. Whether you're playing peek-a-boo with a baby or creating an elaborate pirate fantasy with a four-year-old, these children know we're doing something fun and want to be a part of it. Use play and toys to your advantage – they are great learning aids as well as good distractions after a child does something they are not sure of, like a first submersion. The more involved your child is in the game, the less likely he is to realize that he is trying something new that might be daunting.

KEYS TO AN OPTIMAL LEARNING ENVIRONMENT

To ensure that your child has the best possible environment in which to learn to swim, follow these guidelines:

◎ the parent should always be in the water. This provides instant security and familiarity and promotes trust and bonding

◎ have frequent lessons. Repetition and practice encourage smooth, consistent learning that closely resembles a baby's natural learning pattern

◎ warm, clear water is essential for baby swimming. Babies do not have a fully developed thermal regulatory system so the water needs to be warm. Good water quality also ensures health and safety. (See Choosing a Suitable Pool, pp22–23)

◎ develop a positive learning environment. Create an atmosphere that appeals to the senses by using water play activities, games, songs and colourful toys (see Toys and Learning Aids, pp28–29).

Encouraging toddlers

Once your baby begins evolving into a toddler, signs of emerging independence may challenge your parenting skills and require more patience both in the pool and at home. During this developmental stage the operative word is "No", and "no" may truly mean "no" or it may mean "yes" or even "maybe". It is important at this stage not to make the pool a battleground, as pushing a child who is pushing you usually backfires. Instead, increase the amount of play and slapstick in your routine, and use games, distractions and rapidly changing, entertaining lessons to keep this age group motivated and interested.

Communicating with your child

Think about how you phrase things, and always talk about what you are going to do in a positive rather than a negative way. For example, ask your child to "Jump and splash me and get me all wet", rather than saying, "Jump to me, the water's not going to hurt you." Always appeal to a child's sense of fun and humour — for example, dripping water on the face can be called a "fishy kiss". Remember to always praise every achievement, however small.

If you want to stop your child from doing something, then don't just say "no", but use another tactic. For example, if he is jumping before you finish the count, ask him to count aloud with you, then jump.

Imaginary play Encourage older children to try new skills through imaginary play. For example, diving for a pirate's hidden treasure trove sounds far more exciting than simply diving for rings.

HOW CHILDREN DEVELOP

Every child develops at her own pace, but there are common developmental stages that all children pass through. The exercises in this book are set out according to these stages, so your child will never be learning water skills that she is not yet ready to acquire.

Whether your child is a six-month-old baby who loves the water and swims like a dolphin, or a three-year-old whose mood changes daily about whether she likes the water or not, you need to be aware of what she is physically capable of and the best way to teach her.

BABIES FROM SIX TO 12 MONTHS

The majority of babies of this age group love the water – they enjoy their bathtime and make the transition from bath to pool happily. They are content with water poured in small amounts over their heads and faces, which makes the water-adjustment phase easier and briefer than for older babies.

What to expect in the pool

Babies up to nine months love to splash and wriggle in the water, and show the rapid whole-body undulation of the dolphin- or frog-like reflex kick. Between six and 12 months the reflex kick fades away and is replaced by gliding for a while, until a learned kick is acquired later.

Babies may stare a great deal, but as their age increases you begin to see a more alert and focused child. Learning the Breath-holding Cue (see pp60–61) also shows parents the difference between a reflex reaction and a skill that the child actually learns.

Younger babies also tend to be more sensitive to water temperature. They can become chilly faster, tire more quickly and sleep much longer after swimming.

The benefits of swimming

For nearly all of this age group, baby swimming will be the first educational experience out of the home environment, and it is important to make it a positive one. In general, parents of younger babies tend to be nervous when taking their child swimming, but don't worry, as you will find that your baby is very durable, and that both of you are very capable.

Within this age group lies the golden opportunity to become at home on, in and under the water quite easily. The young baby is still close to the fluid environment she left in the womb, she has no fears and is not yet claiming independence. Once babies are comfortably swimming at this young age, they will never know a time when they didn't know how to swim. They will not be afraid of the water and can learn safety skills sooner than children who start at an older age.

TODDLERS FROM ONE TO THREE YEARS

Sturdy legs, an evolving kick, increased coordination and a sense of humour typifies this age group of swimmers. This broad age span includes beginner walkers to running toddlers; non-verbal babblers to competent speakers; and easygoing one-year-olds to independence-testing three-year-olds.

Because of their interest in manipulating toys and objects, as well as the fact that they can understand the games and observe actions and consequences, children of this age are prime participants for learning through interactive games and songs.

What to expect in the pool

Because the age range is so large, so is temperament. Starting swimming at 13 to 18 months means you'll still be in a primary period of receptivity to water, making it easier to learn how to swim – there will be less fear, more cooperation, and a love of water. From 19 months to three years, growing independence, stubbornness and fear may necessitate clever game playing, humour and additional time for your child to learn new skills.

As most children in this age range are becoming mobile, the early reflex kick is now replaced by a learned and voluntary kick.

The benefits of swimming

Children of this age begin to be more aware of each other and will copy other children, so for beginner and intermediate swimmers this is a good time to start swimming with other children. Through playing games and using toys together in the pool, children develop social skills such as sharing and communication.

CHILDREN FROM THREE TO FOUR YEARS

These children are real characters and make swimming lessons lively with their burgeoning personalities, highly verbal commentary and vivid imaginations. They are fun to interact with, and have their own particular likes and dislikes as well as varying experiences of the water.

What to expect in the pool

With physical sturdiness and growing coordination this age group is very capable of swimming well. They can produce a strong voluntary kick and sit, climb or stand with little or no assistance. However, if they are just starting to learn to swim at these ages, a good percentage of children will have fears. Some of these fears may be pronounced and almost paralysing, others slight and easily calmed.

Watching a peer who already swims can bolster confidence, and children like to show their peers and siblings what they can do. Peer learning is extremely appealing at these ages, and if you can gather a group of friends and their parents then you will see the benefits as the children copy and encourage each other. If one child kicks well she

can show off her vigorous splashes, while another might be a great bubble blower, and yet a third may put her face in the water happily.

Children begin to focus more, follow simple directions and link several skills together. Imaginative play also distinguishes this age group and helps both a frightened, hesitant child as well as a boisterous one. Try using a circus, pirate or spaceship theme in your lesson — whatever motivates and encourages your child.

Children in this age group also like to work for rewards. A simple hug may do. Or let her collect a pile of toys earned one at a time as a reward. Little steps, reinforced and repeated again and again, begin to instil a pattern of a desired behaviour.

The benefits of swimming

Part of gaining trust involves respecting a child who tells you that she doesn't want to put her face in the water. Where you as a parent can help her transcend that fear is by using play, games and humour to help her accomplish a submersion in small, non-threatening stages. You may encounter stalling techniques, but be patient. Once they have gone past the largest hurdles, this age group demonstrates great competency.

SIGNS TO STOP

Responding to your baby's needs, health, security and comfort have been part of your job description since the day he was born. Now you need to take your keen nurturing and observational skills to the pool where your parental instincts will help you gauge the flow of instruction and, most importantly, when to slow down or stop.

A TEAR-FREE ZONE

Make your swimming lessons a "tear-free zone". Often people who have witnessed aggressive swimming lessons are astonished at the laughter, water confidence and lack of tears at our school.

There are several ways to keep the mood lighthearted and the learning stress-free, including stopping, going more slowly, or matching your child's pace accurately. You cannot do everything at once in baby swimming, and trying to do so will only stress your child and overwhelm him. Always speak calmly and softly and move gently — a rough tug, hard push or gruff, impatient tone will only lead to tears.

Remember the following points:

◎ do not introduce any new skills until a child is ready

◎ if you see signs of resistance or discomfort because you've jumped ahead of your child's readiness, stop. Go back to the previous skill or portion of the skill and do not move on until your child is ready

◎ don't do everything all at once. Instead, do a little bit each lesson and gradually the skills will develop

◎ if you are stressed or frustrated, stop. Step back and take a deep breath before starting afresh

◎ if your baby is uncomfortably cold, shivering, has blue lips, is tired or upset, stop immediately and exit the pool

◎ lessons should be happy, playful times together. There is no one rushing or timing you, so go at your child's pace and relax. If things aren't going smoothly, just play, enjoy the water for the rest of the lesson and start again at the next session.

SIGNS NOT TO GO IN

There are some days when it is important to stop before you even begin. If your child is physically ill, for example has a bad cold, heavy congestion, a stomach virus with vomiting or diarrhoea, a fever, an ear infection, conjunctivitis or anything contagious or infectious, stay at home and rest until he is better. Not only are you potentially exposing others to illness if you swim, but in some of these cases your child's muscle strength, lung capacity and mood will be compromised by exercise such as swimming. In other cases, your doctor will call a temporary halt to lessons until a successive visit clears your baby to resume activities. Otherwise, use your good judgement and do not take your child swimming until he returns to his normal activity levels and health.

WHEN NOT TO SUBMERGE YOUR CHILD

When first learning the cue for submersions (see pp60–61), some babies may splutter, cough or be a bit surprised. Usually, their attention can be redirected with a toy or different activity. However, if, after a couple of times, your child is uncomfortable or begins resisting the cue and submersion by arching his back, stop. Go back to playing at the Water Pouring Station (see pp46–47) and practising the Cheek Dip (see p58). Once the Cheek Dip has been re-introduced slowly and successfully, you can try the Cheek Roll (see p59). After a couple of weeks, as comfort returns, you can re-attempt the forwards motion of the Breath-holding Cue (pp60–61).

How often to submerge your child

Excessive water swallowing, choking and gagging are not part of this programme, so limit the number of times that you submerge your child each lesson and gradually introduce submersions so that breath holding is learned over a period of lessons. If you feel your baby has swallowed a bit too much water, stop. Slow down and return to the Water Pouring Station (see pp46–47) before gradually re-attempting submersions. Remember, never force your child to go under water.

THE "TERRIBLE TOOS"

Often when parents are having problems teaching their baby to swim it can be traced back to an adult's "Terrible Toos": expecting too much, too soon, too far and too often.

Too much
Babies can easily become overwhelmed, for example by having too much water poured over the top of their heads, or when too much new material is presented to a hesitant child.

Too soon
You should always be alert and aware of signs of readiness in your baby before you attempt new skills. His comfort, competence and relaxed confidence will indicate he is ready to try the next step. Attempting skills that are not age-appropriate will stress babies and result in a lack of trust, an unwillingness to attempt previous skills, frustration and tears. Progress sequentially through the book, waiting to build up the skills as your child grows and develops both physically and mentally.

Too far
When swimming your child under water, don't stand too far from your partner, so your child doesn't have to swim a long way to reach him. Keep your child's trust by lifting him out of the water while he has air in his lungs and is holding his breath comfortably. Lung capacity is gained over time, not in leaps, and swallowing excess water will hurt your child.

Too often
Repetition is the key to reinforcing a new skill, but know when to stop. Putting a young beginner under water too often when he is just learning the Breath-holding Cue (see pp60–61) may mean he tires and begins swallowing water. Asking an apprehensive three-year-old to put his face in too often starts eroding trust. Practise skills, but move on to a new task before overdoing any one skill.

CHOOSING A SUITABLE POOL

Think of the care that you put into looking after your baby, and make sure that this extends to choosing a suitable public pool in which to teach your child to swim. Take your time and check out the pools in your area carefully. The pool and changing rooms must be clean, and the water clean, clear and warm.

POINTS TO CONSIDER

There are a number of important points you should bear in mind (see also Questions and Answers, pp32–33) before you select a pool in which to teach your child:

◎ the pool water should be warm and clean

◎ the poolside area, changing rooms and shower areas should be well-maintained and safe

◎ buggy access should be available, with adequate space on the poolside areas

◎ the poolside area should have good drainage so that it is not slippery

◎ the pool should be of comfortable depths for your lessons (see opposite)

◎ the pool water should be crystal clear

◎ disinfectant levels, for example of chlorine, must be sufficient to eliminate the risk of infection but should not irritate your child

◎ indoor pools should be adequately ventilated so there are no overpowering chemical smells

◎ outdoor pools should have some shade

◎ the lifeguards should be trained in CPR and First Aid and should be helpful, friendly and informative

◎ an emergency telephone should be close by.

As well as the above, make sure that the pool opening times are convenient and that there is safe parking and access to the pool.

Size of pool

Pools come in all shapes and sizes, but with a little creativity you can carve out your own niche and adapt your lesson to any shape of pool. If it is just you and your baby then you will need a minimum area of 2.4 x 2.4m (8 x 8ft); for a small group you need at least 4.6 x 4.6m (15 x 15ft).

Checking the depth

You will feel most comfortable holding your baby in waist- to chest-deep water, the height of which will vary between people, but is usually around 1–1.2m (3¹/2–4ft) deep.

It is best to use an area of the pool with an even depth or a very gradual slope. When working with a slope, just be aware of where — and how rapidly — the drop-off occurs, and try not to teach near any dramatic drop-off so that you don't suddenly enter deep water and lose your footing.

Ladder or step access

Pool steps can be useful for a number of activities. For example, they are the ideal place for helping older children learn to put their faces in the water (see pp80–81). Also the Alligator Walk (see p85) is practised on the steps. Older babies love the independence of standing on the steps, kneeling on their hands and knees, or putting their faces into a shallow area of water.

If there is only ladder entry at your chosen pool then you can still accomplish everything noted above through other activities.

Water cleanliness

The pool water should be clear enough so that you can see the bottom of the pool easily. Your public pool must adhere to the water quality standards set by your local government health officials. Acceptable Ph levels are between 7.2 and 7.8, with 7.4–7.6 as ideal. The levels of disinfectant must be high enough to ensure that the pool water is impeccably clean, but not so strong that they cause visual or respiratory problems. If, when you place your face in the water, the water hurts your eyes then we recommend not swimming in it with your child.

Water temperature

Ideally, the water temperature in the pool should be very warm for babies, and 32–34°C (90–93°F) is optimal. If you have your own pool, then a pool thermometer is an inexpensive and invaluable investment. In a public pool, other swimmers will generally require lower temperatures so you will need to compromise. If the water is less than 29.5°C (85°F), you may need to shorten the length of your lesson.

If your child begins to shiver, has blue lips, is unhappy, or less cooperative than usual, get out of the pool, dry off and warm up. Remember that babies have immature thermal regulatory systems and chill easily.

Outdoor hot tubs and Jacuzzis are also not recommended for use by babies as temperature in these small pools often soar to 39.5°C (103°F), which is dangerous as it far exceeds a baby's normal body temperature of 37°C (98.6°F).

Air temperature

Take note of the air temperature. Remember that the amazing thing about an indoor pool is that you might be swimming in a warm, heated pool while there is snow on the ground outdoors. Even though the water is heated, you'll want the surrounding indoor air to keep you from feeling chilled. The air temperature indoors should be at least 24°C (75°F), which will be a comfortable temperature for you in a dry swimsuit before you enter the pool. Changing rooms should be kept at a comfortable temperature too.

If you are swimming outdoors then it is best to swim when the air is at least 24°C (75°F), with sunny skies and little or no wind, so there is no wind chill.

THE POOL AS A CLASSROOM

When your baby sees your pool classroom, she should get the impression that it is a fun place to learn. Like any conscientious and organized teacher, you should plan a layout of your space and equip your classroom before you begin. First walk the pool you plan to use without your baby. Check for water clarity, appropriate temperature, ease of entry, depths and slope. Imagine where you'll play the games you've planned (see Games and Songs, pp48–51).

SAFETY

Small children lack the cognitive ability to discern danger, and as water holds endless fascination for children of all ages you must take every precaution to prevent your child from entering the pool without you. It is your responsibility to implement safe procedures and prevent impulsive explorers from entering the water unsupervised.

CONSTANT SUPERVISION

It is vital that you never leave a child unattended either in or around water. This applies whether you are at a public pool, a friend's house, at home or on holiday. Remember:

◎ never leave a child unattended in the bath

◎ always know where your children are, especially when you are near a body of water

◎ never assume someone else is watching your child

◎ make sure that other caregivers understand the importance of constant supervision

◎ maintain constant eye supervision with your child when around water

◎ teach your child never to go in or near the water without a parent or caregiver

◎ if your child begins to walk or run towards the pool without you, call to her emphatically to wait for you, then calmly but quickly walk over to her and take her hand in yours

◎ if your child is missing, always check the pool or other bodies of water first

◎ do not drink alcohol when supervising children

◎ keep contact with your baby when in the water.

BE PREPARED

Familiarize yourself with recognized pool safety standards and teach your children all the pool and water safety rules. Good safety habits, acquired early on, will last a lifetime. Remember that prevention is always the best cure, and that no child should ever be considered "drownproof".

Before you start your lessons, prepare an Action Plan so that you know what to do in case of an emergency. This will help you to react quickly, calmly and effectively if something untoward happens to your child.

Whether in a public or private pool, always check first that the pool is safe, that no area is overly slippery and could cause a child to fall into the pool and that the water is clean and clear.

At a public pool:

◎ check that the poolside area, changing rooms and shower areas are safe and well-maintained

◎ ensure you know where the lifeguards and emergency telephone are, as well as the rescue poles or ring buoys

◎ check that the lifeguards are trained in CPR and First Aid.

At a home pool:

◎ have a rescue pole and ring buoy by the pool

◎ take toys and other appealing objects out of the pool and pool area when not in use

◎ keep a telephone by the pool, and make sure that emergency numbers are stored in the phone's memory.

LEARNING SWIMMING SAFETY SKILLS

No method of baby swimming can guarantee that your child will not drown, but by learning to swim she will increase her chance of getting to safety if she finds herself in the water in an unsupervised situation. The following safety skills should only be taught at the appropriate age and only when your child is ready. To maintain the efficiency of the safety skills, you should reinforce them at least twice a week as part of a 30-minute lesson. Start by teaching your child the first skill, and build up a foundation for the next skill.

With proper prerequisites and training:

At eight months a baby can begin to learn to hold her breath and propel herself through the water with confidence. This gives parents a few valuable seconds if their child enters the water.

At 19 months a capable swimmer can begin to learn to return to the side of the pool. By 24 months, this skill may be executed with ease.

At three years a competent swimmer can begin to learn to lift her head out of the water and take a breath.

At three-and-a-half an experienced swimmer can begin to learn to back float and roll from her front to her back and then her back to her front.

CPR AND FIRST AID

We strongly recommend that parents and caregivers are certified in Infant/Child CPR, First Aid and Water Safety. Courses in these skills are run by recognized organizations (see Resources, p124).

Having a sturdy, high fence around your garden and a good mesh-type pool fence that children cannot climb over are essential safety requirements if you have a home pool.

BARRIERS AROUND A HOME POOL

The abilities of infants and toddlers change from day to day, so make sure that you have layers of protection to prevent your child from accidentally entering the pool area. Remember that a young child can drown in just a few centimetres of water, so if you are visiting a pool without child-proof barriers, always make sure that you can see where your child is. If your child is missing, always check the pool or other bodies of water first.

◎ Close and lock all entrances from the house to the pool, spa or other body of water.

◎ Install an extra lock at the top of any doors leading to the pool. This should be well above the reach of children.

◎ Completely surround the pool with a mesh-type fence. This must be impenetrable by children from all sides. It should have a high degree of transparency and a child-resistant lock. Always keep the gate closed and locked when the pool is not in use. If you use a different kind of fence, make sure that children will not be able to get a foothold and climb over it.

◎ Install a pool alarm. Some of these detect motion; others detect a mass in the water.

◎ Use a safety pool cover. This will totally isolate the pool. Remove the cover completely when the pool is in use.

◎ If you have an above-ground swimming pool, secure, lock or remove any steps when the pool is not in use.

◎ Install a perimeter fence or wall around your garden to stop unauthorized access by children from the outside.

WHAT YOU NEED – THE BASICS

We suggest that you pack a swimming bag for your baby and restock it after each lesson. As well as a swimsuit, towel and swimming nappies, don't forget to take sunblock, ear drops, a change of clothes and a snack for your child.

SWIMSUIT

Your child's swimsuit should fit comfortably and have snug elastic around the legs for girls, and waist and legs for boys. Rinse and dry the suit after swimming.

SWIMMING NAPPIES

Non-toilet-trained babies should always wear a swim nappy, and in some countries this must be worn with a swimsuit. You can use either a re-useable, washable swim nappy, or a specially designed disposable swim nappy. For older children, you could use a swimsuit with a built-in nappy or liner. Unlike regular disposable nappies, which aren't suitable for swimming, disposable swim nappies will not break apart in the pool, nor will they absorb pool water and weigh your baby down. The two layers

OPTIONAL EXTRAS

As your lessons progress, you may want to add some extra items to your swimming bag (see Resources, pp124–25).

◎ A silicone swim cap. This slips easily on and off a baby's head without tugging at her hair.

◎ A neoprene wetsuit for cold weather.

◎ Mesh and rubber pool shoes for use with flexible rubber fins (flippers).

◎ Goggles. Buy anti-fog, anti-leak goggles that fit snugly on your child's face.

of protection – the swim nappy and the swimsuit – should contain any accident and give you time to get your child out of the pool to change him. It is a good idea to take a spare nappy to the pool.

SUNBLOCK

If swimming outdoors, you will need to apply a high-factor waterproof child's sunblock. To maximize protection, apply to exposed areas half-an-hour before entering the pool. This allows time for the sunblock to be absorbed thoroughly into the skin and it will be less likely to run into your child's eyes. As sunblock stings and irritates the eyes, be very careful how you apply it.

WHAT PARENTS NEED

You will require a serviceable, baby-proof swimsuit that won't fall off when your child tugs it, waterproof sunblock, a towel and a change of clean, dry clothes.

When you take your baby swimming always use swim nappies because regular nappies will simply disintegrate in the water.

You may want to purchase a sun-protective suit (see Resources, pp124–25) for your child to use for outdoor swimming in sunny climates, or for fair-skinned children. It should be made of fabric that has ultraviolet protection. These suits not only stop the sun's rays, but also help to block the wind

Apply sunblock 30 minutes before you enter the pool so that it soaks into the skin. Remember to reapply it regularly

Pack everything you need in a mesh swimming bag. Make sure you have a large, dry towel, sunblock, ear drops and a snack for your child

Goggles help to protect against the effects of pool chemicals, and can benefit hesitant children greatly. Children over the age of three are most likely to keep googles on

Fins are used to improve kicking and help young swimmers to get the feel of the water. They also help to position the feet correctly, near the surface of the water

Swimmer's ear drops will evaporate any water left in the ear after swimming. Put two to three drops in each ear after swimming. (See also p33.)

TOYS AND LEARNING AIDS

Visit any good early education centre and you will see that toys, songs and games are used to create a stimulating environment. A watery classroom should be no different – so use these suggestions for toys and aids to help your child learn to swim. Don't worry if you don't have everything, as you can improvise with other toys and household equipment.

Toys are a vital component of this swimming programme (see Resources, pp124–25). They can be used to encourage a child to do an activity, as a reward, or as a distraction after trying a new technique. Depending on the pool you are using and your mode of transport, you can either kit out your classes with everything shown below or take just a few things with you in a bag when you go to the pool, such as your child's favourite floating toys and balls, a bucket, a colander or small watering can and some dive rings.

TOYS FOR BEGINNERS
Floating toys and balls can be used to encourage your child to swim towards you and, along with buckets and a floating baby pool, are used in a number of games. Noodles are good for balancing on, while dive rings are fun to duck underwater for.

AIDS FOR INTERMEDIATES
Barbells, hoops, goggles, fins and kickboards are best used by intermediate and older swimmers who have mastered the basic skills.

basketball hoop

mesh bag and towel

buckets

noodles

dive rings and toys

Use a variety of toys every lesson, either as an enticement to swim towards, a reward, or as a distraction for your child after he attempts a new skill.

Wearing fins (top) not only lets your child swim further, but helps to tone and condition the leg muscles.

Swimming through a hoop (above) provides a focus for your child and encourages proper body alignment.

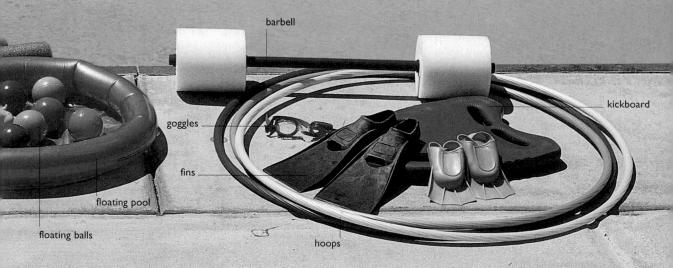

barbell

kickboard

goggles

fins

floating pool

floating balls

hoops

QUESTIONS AND ANSWERS

PARENTAL CONCERNS

I can't swim, and I'm afraid of the water. Can I still teach my baby to swim?

As long as you can stand comfortably in waist- to chest-deep water, you'll have no problem. You don't need to go under water or be able to swim in order to teach your child. Just act confidently and happily so you don't transfer any anxieties you may have to your child. Often, non-swimming parents who witness the joy of baby swimming become relaxed enough to give swimming another chance.

I am nervous about teaching my baby on my own. What can I do?

How about asking a group of like-minded friends, relatives or neighbours and their babies to join you? Not only will you feel happier with the support of other adults in the water, but the group energy is contagious and puts everyone in a happy, playful, encouraging mood. Babies are taught in group classes at our swimming school as we find children learn best when swimming with other children.

Who can substitute for me in the water if I can't get in the pool with my baby?

Your child will succeed best when she has a trusted, familiar caregiver with her in the pool – for example, an uncle, grandparent or babysitter. Just make sure that your substitute fully understands the gentle nature of this child-centred approach and follows the teaching instructions carefully.

I'm pregnant. Can I still teach my baby to swim?

At any one time, nearly a quarter of the mothers in our swimming school are pregnant. As long as you get clearance from your doctor, there is no reason why you shouldn't give your child swimming lessons.

I want to take my baby to swimming lessons as well as teaching her myself, but how do I choose a good one?

There are a number of highly recommended classes with good reputations, but you should still make sure the class meets your criteria for your child. We recommend group classes as children benefit from watching and playing with

their peers. Make sure that there is a positive atmosphere with songs, games and happy babies, and that there is a good rapport between the teacher, children and parents. The teacher should be patient, enthusiastic and focused on their class, knowing when and how to introduce skills gradually and sequentially in the curriculum and at the child's level of readiness.

AGE-RELATED QUERIES

Do I really have to wait for my baby to be six months before I start teaching her to swim?

In our experience, starting formal instruction when your child is at least six months old is sensible. She has a medical history by six months, her head and neck strength have improved and her level of alertness has increased. Plus, you have gained a comfort level in caring for your child. There's also a lot you can do prior to six months to prepare her for her first swimming lessons (see Bathtime Fun, pp38–39).

My daughter is nearly four. Am I too late to start teaching her to swim?

It is never too late to learn how to swim! We like to start babies before 19 months as younger babies usually love the water and are not testing their limits (nor their parents') as toddlers often are. For older children, fear may be more of a factor due to the child's increased understanding of her physical world, her actions and the concept of danger. However, it is a thrill to teach beginner three- and four-year-olds. They may require more patience, more play and more trust building, but their imaginations are developing, they are more verbal, their sense of humour can be tapped and their pride once they learn something as momentous as swimming is incredible to watch. It may take your older baby longer to adjust to the water and learn the initial skills, but once she gains her confidence, her more mature physical abilities, coordination and ability to comprehend and follow directions will allow her to move through the programme more rapidly than a younger baby would.

My three-year-old is so stubborn. How will I ever teach her to swim?

Start by simply playing. Use toys, songs and games to demonstrate what fun the two of you will have in the water (see Games and Songs, pp48–51). Don't make the pool a battlefield – make it fun with lots of toys, balls, cups and colanders she can play with and manipulate. Concentrate at first on things she finds interesting, then once you establish a learning rapport, you can slowly incorporate new skills into your play.

THE BEST WAY TO LEARN

How often should we take our baby swimming?

"A little bit on a lot of days" is best. The more frequently you swim with your baby, the more natural the learning will be. Watch how your baby practises crawling at home and note how she learns a little bit every day and tries again and again, improving as time progresses. Because a baby can't swim in the pool by herself, you need to build her consistent, frequent lessons into your schedule. We have found that in baby swimming, particularly at the start, optimal learning consists of practising four times per week, for 30 minutes each session, over a course of weeks and

months, gradually adding and refining skills. For frightened children or those who have had a bad water experience, four lessons per week is essential for overcoming apprehension and slowly building trust and comfort.

What happens if I can't take my child swimming as often as you suggest I should?

Many busy family schedules do not permit four days of practice per week, but if you can visit the pool at least twice a week the learning will progress smoothly over a more extended and gradual time-frame. As you will be spending less time in the pool practising skills, you should try to have additional bathtime sessions during the week to reinforce the pool lessons through songs and water play.

When is the best time to practise?

Babies learn best when they are comfortable, rested, alert and fed. Choose a time halfway between sleep times, for example during the morning or early evening. Sleep times vary and they often change for individuals during the course of learning to swim. This is normal and can be due to age, developmental growth, change of schedule or even the seasons, so adjust your swimming lessons accordingly. Try not to have to wake a sleeping baby for a swimming lesson, as your child is likely to be cranky and uncooperative. You can feed your baby before your lesson, but make sure you don't start swimming with her for at least half-an-hour after you have fed her.

Can I use toys, songs and games in my lessons, or will they distract my child?

We use toys to our benefit – as motivation, a reward or a distraction to redirect attention. By using toys your child will learn about manipulating his environment – while playing at the Water Pouring Station (see pp46–47), he will discover which objects float, which sink and how liquid conforms to the container it fills. Songs provide a needed diversionary break or rest following busier, more active exercise. Songs and games also enhance child development on many levels, including helping the development of motor skills and tactile stimulation. (See also Toys and Learning Aids, pp28–29, and Games and Songs, pp48–51.)

Can I vary how often I teach my child?

Once a beginner has established his foundation skills, ideally by having four lessons a week, switching to the twice-a-week format for intermediate and advanced skills is often easier to sustain for busy families. By this point, your child will be familiar with the structure of the lesson and all its elements. However, remember that if you go to the pool less often, you will need to adjust your teaching methods and introduce new skills more slowly. You may also find that only going twice a week is not providing enough water time, exposure, or practice for your child, and if this is the case, then increase the number of times you go. In addition, if your child is very clingy or apprehensive, going swimming more often will result in a better, more relaxed, natural atmosphere for him.

Can I use inflatable armbands, buoyancy trainer swimsuits or flotation devices?

Various swimming aids are acceptable if used solely as a supplement to your lessons, but several problems exist with their use. First, if you put your child in a flotation device (armbands, tube, buoyancy swimsuit or similar), you must remain within hand's reach of him. These items are not lifesaving devices and a child may get in trouble if not watched carefully. Second, all of these devices are ultimately designed to keep your child's head out of the water. Because we are trying to teach a flat, horizontal position with your child's face in the water, this awkward position with the head out of the water can establish technique problems or bad habits that must then be overcome. On the plus side, when

used as supplements to your lessons, these devices can provide an alternative way for your child to play in the pool, and may encourage kicking and water adjustment.

SAFETY CONCERNS

How can I choose a good pool to take my baby to?

Make sure that the pool and changing facilities are well-maintained, clean and safe, and that the water is clear and warm (32–34°C/90–93°F is best). The water should be disinfected so that it is clear, not cloudy, but there shouldn't be an overwhelming smell of chemicals. Check if or where the pool slopes into the deep end, and make sure you know where the lifeguards are located. (See also Choosing a Suitable Pool, pp22–23.)

How soon can I teach my baby water safety rules?

Because young babies comprehend language before they can actually speak, you can start shaping safety practices and setting pool rules very early on. In this book, you will

see that children are taught not to jump until the count of "three". Waiting for the count of "three" is critical as it reinforces the fact that pool entry requires adult permission and does not just happen when the child wants it to. Once your baby starts to walk, begin establishing a simple routine. Never let your child walk towards the pool without you, but take his hand in yours and walk together. This early repetition will often result in your child actually seeking out your hand prior to approaching the pool. (See also Safety, pp24–25, and Learning to Wait, p76.)

There is so much concrete in and around pools, how can I protect my baby from bumps and scrapes?
Hard surfaces can spell potential accidents. When by the pool, practise walking, rather than running, with your child towards the pool. Verbally point out the fact that, "We walk, not run, when going to the pool." Avoid obviously slick or wet surfaces if you are carrying your child. Once in the pool, practise unaided swims in open areas away from walls. When practising swims for which you approach the wall, move more slowly and deliberately. Your adult walking pace towards the wall will allow your child to swim at the actual speed he kicks in the water and will avoid accelerating him towards concrete surfaces.

HEALTH-RELATED CONCERNS

Should my baby be inoculated before swimming classes or prior to entering a public pool?
Just as you would do for any other physical activity, your child should be cleared by your doctor before enrolling in swimming classes, or before you begin teaching him at home. By the age of six months, most babies have received preliminary inoculations. Before you go swimming, also make sure that you and your child are free of contagious diseases and that neither of you has open cuts or sores.

My baby has a cough and runny nose – can we still go swimming together?
It is not normally advisable to go swimming if your baby has a cold, as he will have a harder time holding his breath and exercising, and he may not feel like going in the water at all. Just rest at home until he feels better. On your return to the water, take it easy; his skills may be a little rusty.

Can premature and physically or mentally challenged babies learn to swim?
The forgiving buoyancy of water and the gentleness of this programme, coupled with the focus on parental bonding, is outstanding therapy. We have taught premature infants, babies who are developmentally delayed or have autism or Down's Syndrome, and babies with physical limitations or muscular weaknesses – all have thrived in the water. Just check with your doctor before you start lessons.

If my child has asthma or allergies can I take him swimming, or will it make his condition worse?
As always, you must clear all pre-existing medical conditions with your doctor before starting swimming lessons. Some research has found that swimming may be less likely to produce symptoms in children with asthma than other forms of exercise. This is thought to be because the humid air in the pool area doesn't irritate the respiratory system as much as dry air does. Generally, very few allergies are triggered by swimming, although there are a few children who are sensitive to chlorine.

Is my child likely to develop an ear infection as a result of swimming?
If you take preventative measures – using ear drops after each swim – your child is unlikely to get a swimmer's ear infection. As a baby can't unclog a water-blocked ear, it will be your measures that will make sure trapped water doesn't turn into a bacterial ear infection. Buy ready-made ear drops from a chemist and put two or three drops in each ear after swimming.

How can I tell if my baby has an ear infection?
If your child tugs at his ear or tries to put his finger in his ear and is irritable, he may have swimmer's ear (otitis externa) and you should take him to see your doctor. If treatment is required then do not take your child swimming until the problem has cleared up. The other common ear infections are middle ear infections (otitis media), which seem to be unrelated to swimming and result from colds, congestion, allergies etc. Your doctor will advise you whether your child can swim. If frequent ear infections have necessitated "tubes" being placed in his ears, consult your doctor about the measures you should take.

WATER CONFIDENCE

Come on in... the water's waiting! Whether your baby is just six months
or nearly four years old, this chapter shows you enticing learn-through-play
strategies to teach him essential foundation skills. From early fun and play
in the bath to entering the pool safely, holding your child in the
water and using toys, games and songs, this chapter prepares you
for your first lessons. The initial step is water adjustment, in which
your baby learns to be comfortable in the pool. Then, based on
his readiness, you'll teach him to hold his breath when submerging
on cue. With time, practice and proficiency, you'll let go of him for
a solo swim. Finally, you will witness the event that is the goal of
this chapter – your baby swimming freely between his parents
for five seconds – a wonderful achievement.

TEACHING BEGINNERS

Parents of all beginners, whether six months or four years old, should start here. Some of you may have never taken your child to a pool, some may have played with your baby in the water or even submerged your child. Whatever level you are at, start at the beginning of the programme and gradually, with practice, your child will gain confidence in the water.

BATHTIME FUN

Even before your first trip to the pool, get your child accustomed to water during her bath (see pp38–39). If she loves the water, we want to keep it that way; if she doesn't care for it, we want to improve the situation. Remember the key approaches of the programme — long-term, gradual, child-centred, playful, developmentally and age-appropriate — and put these into practice in the bath.

WATER ADJUSTMENT

Getting your child used to the water, and helping her to learn to love it is a key part of this programme. The first stage of water adjustment happens in the bath. Once your child is happy playing in the bath, you can transfer your bathtime games and songs to the pool.

In the pool, introduce water on your own face or on a doll or puppet, then try a little on your child's face. Play at the Water Pouring Station (see pp46–47), which is a fun way to get her accustomed to the water. Always make sure your child is happy in the pool. If she becomes distressed and cannot be distracted by a toy or game, stop. Back off and simply play games or pour water on less threatening parts of the body than the face and head.

Play is a great way for your child to become comfortable with having water poured or splashed onto her. Games and songs (pp48–51) are therefore ideal tools for water adjustment as well as for learning new skills. Attention spans are short at these ages, so to keep your child happy in the pool make sure your lessons flow well. By following the format of the Activity Circuit (see pp52–53) your child will practise different skills as she moves at her own pace from one activity to another.

USING THE LESSON PLANS

Lesson plans are given at the start of each stage of the skills for beginners. These are suggestions for fast-paced 30-minute lessons, allowing you to practise the skills you teach your child in fun, inviting ways. By following the plans, your child will practise a wide range of skills without you losing her attention. The structure of the plans and the focus on the routine of the Activity Circuit also bring familiarity and consistency to your swimming sessions, so your child will come to look forward to each successive part of the lesson.

When you start teaching your child to swim, simply play with her in the water, then, once you feel she is ready, introduce the exercises in Stage One one at a time as listed in the lesson plan. Remember that your child will be able to practise only a few of the skills, so spend plenty of time playing games or at the Water Pouring

Station during your lessons. Over time, she will master all the skills in Stage One, and you will be able to complete the entire lesson plan for that stage, and can move on to the next. Amend the lesson plans slightly each session to suit your child's mood on the day.

BEGINNERS: WHERE TO START

All beginners should start the programme at Beginners: Stage One (pp54–69), regardless of their age, because the general foundation skills that all young swimmers need are introduced here. Start off slowly, spending time getting your child adjusted to the water using games, songs and play, keeping your lessons as fun as possible. Work through the exercises sequentially at your child's pace, practising the skills by following the Stage One lesson plan (p55).

BEGINNERS AGE SIX TO 11 MONTHS

If your child is between six and 11 months old, start with Beginners: Stage One (pp54–69). Once she has mastered all the skills given in this section, and turns one year old, you can move on to teach her the new skills given in Beginners: Stage Two (pp70–77). When she has learned the skills in Stage Two and is at least 14 months old, move on to the Intermediates chapter (pp86–123).

BEGINNERS AGE 12 TO 35 MONTHS

If your child is aged between one year and 35 months then start with Beginners: Stage One. Once she can perform all the skills given in that section, move on to Beginners: Stage Two to help her build on the foundation skills learned in Stage One. Once your child has acquired all the foundation skills in Stages One and Two and is at least 14 months old, move on to the Intermediates chapter.

BEGINNERS AGE THREE TO FOUR YEARS

If your child is aged between three and four years, you should first refer to the section showing Adaptations for Three- to Four-year-old Beginners (pp78–85). This section has its own lesson plan that uses many of the techniques shown in Beginners: Stage One, but — importantly — it substitutes Stage One submersion skills (pp59–62) with self-submersions (pp80–81) which are more age-appropriate. Also, the swims in Stage One (pp64–67) are replaced by the techniques on pp82–83.

Once your child has mastered all the self-submersions and swims specifically adapted for three- to four-year-olds successfully, and has learned other Stage One foundation skills (kicking, jumping and balance), she can move on to Beginners: Stage Two.

BATHTIME FUN

If your baby enjoys his bathtime, we want to maintain and transfer his love of water to the pool where play is broader, splashes are bigger and water is everywhere on the horizon. For a baby less enchanted by the bath and having water on his face, going to the pool will get him used to water in a different environment. By using your baby's daily bath routine to bring in play that complements swimming, you elevate a simple daily ritual into an essential learning tool.

As your baby's view expands beyond the confines of his bath and you both develop new ways to interact with water, baths become easier and more pleasurable. Months of preparation in the bath before beginning baby swimming will help you and your child move smoothly from the bath to the pool.

First baths – sponge bathing

A baby's first baths are generally not done in the bath, but by sponge bathing. Early bathtimes should be loving moments spent interacting with your baby. A soft tone of voice, gentle singing and warm water squeezed from a flannel or sponge, or poured from your hands lets your baby know how special your time with him and the water is. To get your child used to the water, before using soap, trickle water all over him.

Lay your child back very slightly from vertical, and with a cupped hand, cradle his head at the neck. With your other hand, use a wet sponge or flannel to squeeze water gently over the top of his scalp so it flows over his face. If he becomes startled, reassure him with your voice and stroke his arms, cheek, and hair to comfort him. Apply a little water several times each bathtime.

Baths – parent and child

Initially, when your baby moves from sponge baths to the bath you should join him. Before you get in, always test the temperature with your elbow to check it is comfortably warm. Cradle your child securely against you and hold him with one hand. With your other hand, use a flannel or sponge to drizzle water over his head and face. Move him around slowly in the water, supporting his chin and neck with your hands if he is on his stomach, or supporting his neck and head if he is on his back.

Once your baby is older and has head and neck strength, sitting positions will be more interesting for him. It is a good idea to add a selection of colourful floating toys to the bath that he can play with.

At this point, you can also start using songs to encourage water adjustment. First, sing simple songs with verses that encourage hand and feet movements, such as "The Wheels on the Bus" and "If You're Happy and You Know It". Clap, splash and kick with your baby to the various verses. Then, before using soap or shampoo, sing bath-related rhymes such as "This is the Way We Wash our Clothes" (using "Here We Go Round the Mulberry Bush", but substituting body parts for clothes) and dripping small amounts of water over the different parts of your baby as you progress through the verses of the song. Finish by dripping water over the top of his head, then divert your child's attention immediately with a toy.

Baths – older children

Older, stronger babies can sit up on their own in the bath, but never leave a child unattended in the bath, even if he is in only a few centimetres of water. Sit next to the bath so you can watch and interact with your child. This is a good time to introduce a variety of toys with different uses, such as cups for pouring, a waterproof doll you can pour water over, a sieve or colander you can pour water through and a spray bottle you can mist water from. Your baby will be interested in the movement of water from one container to another, and should be encouraged to pour water from the containers onto a doll and himself. This type of play in the bath is a good precursor for the Water Pouring Station (see pp46–47).

SHOWERS

The convenience of showers and the feel of constantly running water on the skin makes them popular with adults, but what about with babies? Showers offer water in a playful way that both you and your child can enjoy. However, they don't allow for time to play with toys the way a bath does, so make sure you build in some fun time. Use a removable shower head to tickle the toes, tummy and fingers, or to drench a puppet or toy.

SAFETY PRECAUTIONS
◎ Turn on the shower before entering and carefully check the water temperature before exposing your baby to it.
◎ Adjust the flow from the shower head to a much more gentle pressure for your baby than would be used by an adult.
◎ Watch that you don't over-expose your child's ears, nose and mouth to rushing water.

From the age of about three, more elaborate fantasy play is possible in the water. Toys should reflect this change, so try adding a mermaid doll and a school of toy fish; a port with boats and cargo; or a troupe of puppets to the bath. As you play with your child develop different scenarios, and make sure you pour water over the toys and your child as you play. Use the puppets to show your child a new trick of blowing bubbles, or dip the mermaid's face into the water and encourage your child to copy her. Children will perform actions for toys and puppets that they would never easily attempt for their parents.

Once your child is at least six months old, enjoys his time in the bath and is happy with water trickling over his head and face, you can take him for his first trip to the pool.

FIRST TRIP TO THE POOL

Before your first trip to the pool, get your child used to the water while in the bath
(see Bathtime Fun, pp38–39). Then, when your child is at least six months old and enjoys
playing in the bath, it's time to transfer your games to the pool.

This is the start of a very exciting journey for both of you, so try to make your child's first experience at the pool a happy one that she'll want to repeat and will begin looking forward to.

Choose an optimal time of day to go to the pool – not one when she is likely to be tired or hungry – and don't rush while you establish a new routine. For your first few lessons, just think of the pool as a "big bath", and let her simply play in the pool and get used to the seemingly vast expanses of water around her.

On your first trip to the pool, allow your child plenty of time to get accustomed to the sights, sounds and smells of this new and strange environment. Remember that she is experiencing a novel and very different location, situation and routine. Observation helps to acclimatize a child, so talk her through the different areas of the pool. Show her the water, toys and changing room. Tell her what a good time you and she are going to have, and how you're going to play together in the pool just like you do in the bath.

Don't pour or trickle any water on your child's face during this initial trip. This is purely a chance for your baby to gain familiarity with the pool and to enjoy the water. This is a great day for observing your baby and bonding with her, and it is therefore vital that you take it slowly and calmly so that she leaves on a positive note and does not have any worries about her next trip to the pool.

During your first few sessions in the pool do not try teaching your child any of the techniques shown further on in this chapter. Practise instead a safe entry into the pool so that you are both happy getting into and out of the water (see pp41–42) and try out a few of the safe holds (see p43). Allow your baby time to get used to the water and the new environment of the pool, practise familiar bathtime activities, some songs and games (see pp48–51), and let her play and relax.

SAFE POOL ENTRY

Getting into and out of the pool may seem to be a straightforward manoeuvre, but with a baby in your arms and wet, slippery surfaces to negotiate, you need a plan that guarantees safety for both you and your child. Each pool is designed in a different way, but assessing the safest access from the poolside into the water and back out again will make for pleasurable first and final moments of your child's swimming lessons. There are a number of different ways you can enter the pool with a baby or young toddler, depending on the access available, your child's age, and whether you are on your own or accompanied by another adult. If you are alone, do not be afraid to ask for help.

Simple pool entry with two adults

If you are at the pool with a partner, then pool entry is simplified. While you stay on the side with your baby, steadying her in a sitting position at the pool's edge, your partner can get into the pool safely. Once he is standing on the pool floor facing your child, you can ease your baby into his arms with either a sitting jump or a lift before entering the pool yourself. Reverse this procedure to carry out a safe exit from the pool.

Simple pool entry with one adult

If you are on your own with a young baby of manageable weight, a safe entry can be accomplished easily down a set of concrete pool steps. With one arm, hold your baby so that he is straddling your hip at the waist. With your free hand, grasp the handrail firmly and walk slowly down the pool steps. If there is no handrail, use your free hand to help you keep your balance if necessary.

Alternate pool entry

Stand with your child next to you by the edge of the pool, with her on your dominant side (your right side if you are right-handed). Carefully lower yourself to a sitting position, with your knees bent and your feet in the water. Help your child to sit next to you in the same position. Tell her to stay seated while you get into the pool, and to wait until you tell her she can jump in.

To enter the pool, place your hands on the pool edge on either side of your hips, with your palms facing down and your fingers facing the water. Push down on your hands, lock your elbows, lift your buttocks and glide into the water gently, so you land standing on the pool floor. Turn so you are standing in front of your child. Place your hands under her armpits so she can jump into your arms.

If you are teaching your child in a pool with no concrete steps, or if you are alone without the benefit of a helping hand, practise the alternate pool entry (see above). Use this only at the shallow end of the pool and with older children who can sit steadily and move independently from a sitting to a standing position and back again.

Throughout this entry, talk to your child so that she knows what you are doing at each point – that you will enter the water first, and that it will then be her turn to get into the swimming pool. This should stop her from trying to get into the water before you are ready to catch her.

Do not attempt the alternate pool entry if your physical abilities are compromised in any way, for example by pregnancy, back problems, or wrist, arm or shoulder weakness.

ENTERING THE POOL SAFELY

◎ Never jump or slide into a pool with a child in your arms.

◎ If unassisted, try to avoid climbing down a ladder when holding a child.

◎ Always use a handrail when one is available.

◎ Move slowly and securely as you enter and exit the pool; there is no rush.

◎ If you are alone or worried, ask pool personnel to help you to enter the water safely.

◎ For the alternate pool entry, choose a depth marked between 90 and 120cms (3 and 4 feet).

SAFE HOLDS

The following holds offer you comfortable and safe options for moving with your child. With all these holds, make sure your hands are secure but relaxed (and not clenched), as this will indicate your confidence. Also, talk to your child throughout to reassure her.

The Waltz Hold

This hold provides the most security for your child, and should be used if he is unsure or clinging to you. It is the ideal hold for the first few trips to the pool. Move a child from the Waltz Hold to the Face-to-face Hold only when you feel him relax in your arms. Hold your baby slightly to one side of your torso, so that he is straddling you around the waist to chest area and is only slightly immersed in the water.

The Face-to-face Hold

You will find that the Face-to-face Hold provides a great opportunity to communicate with your baby as you will have direct eye contact. With your child facing you, place your hands under her armpits, with your thumbs facing up. Walk backwards in the water slowly so that her body floats up and stretches out behind her. Watch her mouth to ensure that she is not licking or swallowing any water. If her mouth is too close to the water, tilt your wrists upwards slightly so that her face moves away from the surface of the water.

The Pass Hold

This is the most common way to hold a relaxed child, and you will use this functional hold to perform most techniques, including kicking drills, passes and swims. Hold your baby on your dominant side (your right side if you are right-handed), so that she is in a near-horizontal position with her face a few centimetres above the water. Your dominant hand should be placed under her far armpit, with your thumb facing up. Your non-dominant hand should be under the armpit nearest to you with your thumb, again, facing up.

WATER ADJUSTMENT

For the first few lessons, simply play in the pool with your child while he becomes accustomed to the water. This is a very important part of the progamme – if your child is comfortable with water streaming down his face, and happy in the pool, he will be able to move on to being submerged under the water easily in later lessons.

Slowly conditioning your child to feel water on his eyes, ears, nose and mouth helps him to adapt gradually to – and later enjoy – the sensation of water on his face when he goes under water. The best way to do this is through play.

Using games

A good way to encourage a child – especially a frightened, older child – to accept the idea of water flowing over his face is to turn it into a game. Use an absorbent foam ball or sponge to stream water playfully over your child's head, or over another object or person. To start with, use only small amounts of water, then increase the amount over the weeks.

For a young baby, pour a trickle of water from a sponge over a doll or puppet, then over your child. Encourage an older baby to sponge water over the doll or puppet, then over himself. With a more confident baby, place the sponge over your own head and let the water drip over your face, reacting gleefully. Then sponge the water over your baby, or let him do it.

If your child is not comfortable with water being poured over his face, begin with pouring games (see pp46–47) until he is more relaxed in the water, then progress to pouring water on his face.

Using songs

Singing a familiar bathtime song helps make the transition from bath to pool a smooth one. Try using "This is the Way We Wash our Clothes" (see p39). Beginning at the toes, move up the body with the next verses, pouring the water over the body part relevant to the verse you are singing. At the verse for the face, take 1/4–1/3 of a cup of water, sing, but before pouring, count "1, 2, 3", then pour the water on to the top of the scalp. Immediately re-direct your child's attention with a toy or different activity.

HELPING FRIGHTENED CHILDREN

For a clinging, fearful baby, the pool can seem like a daunting place, but you can change his perception by building up his trust and confidence in you. Think about how your child might perceive this unfamiliar situation and what he may be worried about. Then think of ways to help your baby to overcome his fears gently. Never pull a clinging child off you, but slowly ease him towards a new level of comfort through play. Some children are so anxious they won't get into the pool for several lessons, but by going slowly you can help.

Start on the steps

Seated, kneeling, or on his stomach, a child in the low-water level of the steps is reminded of his comforting bath. Don't feel like you're missing out on "the big pool" — your baby's face can be submerged from the edge of the steps, he can kick on them, jump from them and slowly ease himself into the bigger spaces.

Basketball fun

The best way to calm a frightened child is to redirect his attention by playing a game — a basketball and floating hoop near the steps are good for this purpose. With both of you standing by the edge of the pool, let your child shoot a hoop and cheer him on. Then move down on to the top step and take alternate turns — you shoot one then he shoots one. Move down the steps gradually when he is ready, continuing to take turns shooting hoops and encouraging him all the time.

USING DISTRACTION TECHNIQUES

When you want to help your child to overcome any apprehensions or worries, try using these distraction techniques:

◎ throw a ball and ask your child to chase after it as you take him through the water towards it. Use whichever hold he is most comfortable with

◎ if there are two of you teaching your child, while you hold him either play a game of catch with a floating ball or encourage him to chase after your partner, who should reward him with a toy when he reaches him (see also p56)

◎ blow bubbles from a jar of toy bubble soap

◎ give him plenty of toys to play with, such as those used in the Water Pouring Station (see pp46–47).

WATER POURING STATION

Encouraging your child to play with water is a great way to get her used to it, whether she is uncertain about having water on her face, or is a beginner swimmer who needs encouragement to go under the water. The Water Pouring Station is great fun and can be set up with any pouring items you have available – children's watering cans, toy waterwheels, cups, kitchen colanders, small buckets, plastic dolls and spray misters are all ideal. Move with your child from one item to the next, both of you pouring water with the objects, into the objects and over each other.

Help your child to pour water over a doll or puppet – this encourages her to pour water over herself, too

Water Play
Choose objects that carry different amounts of water, and from which water can be emptied in different ways, so that your child has plenty of variety to keep her interested

Colanders create a satisfyingly large shower or waterfall of water

WATER ADJUSTMENT THROUGH PLAY

The Water Pouring Station should be used every lesson, whatever your child's abilities, as it has many benefits:

◎ pouring from one vessel to another can help to refine motor skills and coordination

◎ it allows children of different abilities to explore at their own rate in this self-paced activity

◎ it creates a welcome break from skills that might be more intimidating or challenging

◎ it allows you to assess when your child is ready to learn facial submersion. Once a child is comfortable with water streaming over her face, a parent can begin introducing facial submersions and the Breath-holding Cue (see pp60–61).

Cups can be used to pour a sheet of water over the scalp and front of the face

Children love watching water moving as it powers the waterwheel

Watering cans provide a light shower of water, and can be used to pour water over your child, yourself or a doll

Bright, colourful toys and balls are always appealing to children and are reminiscent of bathtime fun

Plastic cups are easy and fun for your child to use. Encourage him to pour water from one cup to another.

GAMES AND SONGS

Treat your first few trips to the pool simply as extra play sessions, allowing your child to become accustomed to the new environment and encouraging a love of water by making the time fun using games and songs. Once you feel your child is ready to start learning the water-confidence techniques (see pp54–85), games and songs will become part of her lessons, keeping her stimulated and happy as she progresses and creating a positive and fun atmosphere that encourages learning.

Just as children love playing at home and at school, so they will love singing and playing games in the water. Games and songs also support learning on a variety of fronts as they involve skills such as coordination, logic and memory. As such, they are invaluable learning aids when you are teaching your child to swim.

Children's songs from around the world lend themselves well to adaptation in the pool. Two of our favourites are "The Wheels on the Bus" and "If You're Happy and You Know It", but use any song that is suitable for the actions involved in water play.

GAMES TO PLAY WITH YOUR CHILD

By integrating games and songs fully into your lessons you will be able to introduce new skills to your baby in entertaining ways. You can also use them to provide fun breaks for your child after she has tried new or challenging skills. Repeat the same games and songs in the bath and the pool so that your child is familiar with them. This will also reinforce the games and accompanying movements and encourage water confidence in both the pool and the bath. Play the games suggested below with your child, but adapt them to suit her and the pool that you are in.

Motor Boat, Motor Boat

Hold your child under her armpits so that she is in the Pass Hold (see p43). Spin yourself and your child around quickly in a circle so that a slight wave is made by your actions. You can just do the spin, telling your child that you are going to go fast like a motor boat does, or even better, you can sing a little song as you play it, first going slowly, then fast, then running out of petrol and stopping. The song goes:

"Motor boat, motor boat go so slow
Motor boat, motor boat go so fast
Motor boat, motor boat, run out of gas!"

Children love to be spun round in the water, making Motor Boat, Motor Boat a very popular game, even with frightened children.

Where Did They Go?

If your child is unsure of being in the water or has been startled when practising one of the water-confidence techniques, show her this "magic trick" to divert her attention.

You will need to fill a bucket with a variety of colourful floating balls and toys. It is easiest to do this trick if you have both hands free, so ideally have a partner in the water to hold your baby.

Show your child the filled bucket, saying, "we're going to play a magic trick", then quickly tip the bucket upside down into the water trapping all the balls inside the submerged bucket. Ask your child, "where did they go?" Then count to three and tip the bucket right side up under the water. All the balls will pop to the surface, and as they do you should shout "there they are!"

Ask your child to pick up the toys and help her to put them back in the bucket so you can play again.

Enjoy the look of delight on your child's face as the balls pop up out of the water when playing Where Did They Go?, then encourage her to fill up the bucket again.

The Pick-a-ball Game

This key game is played every lesson during the Activity Circuit (see pp52–53) and encourages your child to dip, kick or swim under water, depending on her ability — in fact, these skills are introduced as part of this game.

Fill a small inflated baby pool with floating balls and toys and secure it at the edge of the pool. You will also need a bucket on the side of the pool. Ask your child to select a toy. Holding your child, stand opposite your partner, 60–90cm (2–3ft) apart. Ask your child to throw the toy to your partner, then pass her to your partner and the chosen toy. (As your child's comfort in the water increases, submerge or swim her towards your partner using the skills shown on pp58–61 and pp64–67.) As she reaches your partner, he should give her the toy (a good distraction if she is startled at being submerged) and direct her to kick to the pool wall and place the toy inside the bucket. Repeat with the rest of the toys.

TIPS FOR PLAYING GAMES SUCCESSFULLY

◎ Play the same games – or sing the same songs – at home (whether in the garden or the bath). If your child is familiar with them already, she is likely to be confident playing them in the pool.

◎ Choose songs that match movement with lyrics, as these help to stimulate several brain functions at once, helping with the development of gross and fine motor skills, coordination and rhythm.

◎ Interact with your baby while you are playing the games. It will keep her alert and interested and she will follow the concept of what is going on through your running commentary.

◎ If there is a group of you, circle up for singing. It's fun to watch faces across from you doing the motions and may encourage an attempt at a previously untried skill.

GROUP GAMES

While playing group games you will see how much your child benefits from watching his peers, demonstrating what he can do, or copying them. Group games are a great way for children to learn both water and social skills while having so much fun they won't want to stop.

London Bridge is Falling Down

You will need two people to hold two foam noodles in an arch over the water. In a line, parents walk in a large circle, carrying or swimming their child under the noodle bridge while singing "London Bridge is Falling Down". If your child is a beginner, carry him above the water in the Pass Hold (see p43). If your child is comfortable in the water, you can swim him under the bridge either above or under the water, depending on his abilities. On the verse "Take the key and lock her up", the noodles should be dropped to water level so

A very stimulating game, London Bridge is Falling Down is always exciting for young children, who love the combination of the words and actions.

The Pick-a-ball Game is a favourite with children of all ages, and is played several times every lesson as a key part of the Activity Circuit (see pp52–53).

that they encircle a parent-child pair, then raised up again when the main verse is sung. One of the noodle holders may gently pour water from a watering can over the children as they pass under the noodle bridge.

Run and Jump

If you are able to use a large floating mat, which are often available in public pools, then Run and Jump is a good activity for boosting your child's confidence and helping him to learn how to balance on a moving surface. However, as your child will perform a standing jump with a held breath it is only suitable for children who are at the intermediate level (pp86–123).

Working in a group, the parents should line up along one of the long sides of the mat with their children and hold on to the mat with a free hand to stabilize it. On the opposite side, someone with two free hands should "shadow" the child on the mat.

The first parent should lift their child onto the mat, then walk to the end of the mat to wait for their child. The "shadower" should hold the child until the parent is in the catch position, then the shadower should walk or run the child down the mat with one hand under each armpit. While the child runs down the mat have the group chant "run, run, run". When he reaches the end of the mat, the shadower should lift him off the mat, giving him the Breath-holding Cue (see pp60–61) and place him in the water for a dip or swim to the parent. More experienced swimmers will jump in unassisted.

Big Ball Splash

For this game, three or more parents should stand in a circle, holding their children under their armpits so that they are in a vertical position in front of them and facing away from them. Toss a large floating ball into the circle and tell the children to push the ball to their friends. The aim is to get the children to extend their arms, reach forwards and push the ball to another child. When everyone has had a few turns with their hands, ask the children to put their feet up and kick or splash the ball to each other instead.

Everyone has a great time during Big Ball Splash – so much so that they will forget that they are being splashed.

THE ACTIVITY CIRCUIT

Make the Activity Circuit a key part of each lesson as it provides a fun and interactive structure for your child to practise the swimming skills he is learning. The circuit is very flexible and can be adapted to the pool, situation, age and skill level of your child, allowing him to practise different skills at the "stations" that make up the circuit.

We recommend that you use the Activity Circuit every lesson. In it, your child moves around the circuit from one activity to the next, playing different games and practising a wide variety of skills. Its interactive format and use of toys and learning aids provides a lively and fun environment and promotes cognitive, perceptual and sensory-motor development.

The different "stations" of the Activity Circuit provide a set routine for you and your child to practise skills. To benefit most from the circuit, you should devote between 10 and 15 minutes to it in total each lesson, spending just a few minutes at each "station". This means that, depending on your child, you should go round the circuit between three and five times.

Monkey Walk (see p77) Chasing a parent while monkey walking teaches children to move along the pool wall to a safe exit point.

Water Pouring Station (see pp46–47) Here children can get used to water by pouring it over dolls, toys, their parents and themselves.

During the Activity Circuit your child practises key skills such as above- and underwater swims and the Breath-holding Cue (all as part of the Pick-a-ball Game) bringing in new skills as he becomes developmentally ready (see the lesson plans). The Water Pouring Station (see pp46–47) and Pick-a-ball Game (see p49) are key elements of the Activity Circuit.

You can adapt the circuit to suit your child's age and skill level, as well as the pool and the equipment you have. An eight-month-old beginner would play all the games above the water, while an experienced swimmer of three might swim the majority of the course, do standing jumps and dive to find sunken rings.

Each lesson plan outlines the best activities to include in the Activity Circuit for your child's age and ability, although you may need to adapt this plan to suit the pool you are in.

Pick-a-ball Game (see p49) This game incorporates passes and swims in a fun way, with children moving between their parents to retrieve a favourite toy, then dunking it in a bucket.

Basketball (see p28) is a very popular game with children of all ages, and frightened beginners to experienced swimmers love shooting hoops in the pool.

Alligator Walk (see p85) Older children can practise the Alligator Walk, moving along the steps in a way that encourages the correct body alignment for swimming.

BEGINNERS: STAGE ONE
(MINIMUM AGE SIX MONTHS)

STAGE ONE LESSON PLAN

REQUIREMENTS FOR STAGE ONE

Minimum Age: Your child should be at least six months old.

Skill Level: Your child is a beginner. You should have played at home in the bath so she is accustomed to the feel of the water (see Bathtime Fun, pp38–39), and visited and played in the pool to help her adjust to the new environment (see First Trip to the Pool, pp40–43).

All new swimmers should start with this section, whether a water-loving six-month-old baby, a boisterous toddler, or a nervous three-year-old. (Note that there are certain adaptations for three- to four-year-old beginners — see pp78–85.) Once your child is accustomed to playing in the bath, and you have introduced her in an unhurried, non-stressful way to the pool, you can begin using the lesson plan here to structure your 30-minute lessons. These will consist of water-adjustment games as well as the foundation swimming skills given in this section.

Introduce new skills in the order in which they appear in this section. Over the days, weeks and months, move on to the next skill or skill level only when your child masters the skill she has previously learned comfortably. At the end of this stage, your child should be able to complete the lesson plan at the highest skill level listed.

Although the lesson plan is your guideline, always base your lessons on your child's learning ability, mood and comfort levels. Remember that this programme takes a gentle, child-centred approach. Follow your child's lead — if she doesn't want to do one of the techniques one day, don't push her, simply try another that she is familiar with, play a game or spend extra time at the Water Pouring Station (see pp46–47).

LESSON PLAN

WARM UP 3–5 minutes
Practise different holds and kicking.   *pp43; 56*

SONG BREAK 3–5 minutes
Sing "The Wheels on the Bus" or a bathtime song.   *p39*

ACTIVITY CIRCUIT 10–12 minutes total   *pp52–53*
Structure the circuit as shown below. Go around 3–5 times, spending a few minutes at each "station" before moving on to the next.
a) Water Pouring Station   *pp46–47*
b) Jump from the Wall (once per round)   *p63*
c) Pick-a-ball Game (at appropriate level – see below)   *p49*
   This game involves passing your child from one parent to the other. A series of submersion skills are introduced using this pass. Over time, as your child adjusts to one submersion skill, move on to the next in the order given below. Note that some submersions should be practised a maximum of 1–3 times per lesson. As you will be going around the circuit 3–5 times, use the Above-water Pass instead in some circuits so your child isn't submerged too often.
   i) Above-water Pass   *p57*
   ii) Cheek Dip 3–5 times max   *p58*
   iii) Cheek Roll 1–3 times max   *p59*
   iv) The Breath-holding Cue 1–3 times max   *pp60–61*
   v) First Held Underwater Swim 1–3 times max   *pp64–65*
   vi) First Unaided Underwater Swim 3–5 times max *pp66–67*

SONG or GAME BREAK 2–4 minutes
Sing or play one or two songs or games.   *pp48–51*

JUMPS FROM THE WALL 5 minutes total
Jump from the Wall (first or second level depending on ability) 3–4 times max   *p63*

BALANCE 3–5 minutes   *p68*

TIME TO GO 1 minute   *p69*

KICKING

Babies are born with a natural dolphin- or frog-like kicking reflex that usually disappears between six and 12 months and is replaced by a rudimentary learned kick with a small up-and-down movement (a "flutter"). Between the end of the reflex kick and the start of the learned kick there may be no kick at all, and your child will just glide. At this point, if you want to encourage your child to kick, these games are a good way to motivate him.

TEACHING TIPS

When you witness someone else kicking in the pool, point it out to your child, saying "kick, kick".

Praise and reinforce any attempt at kicking, but do not move your baby's legs to simulate a kick.

Tickling a baby lightly on the arch of the foot may prompt a kick.

FIRST OPTION

Stand in waist- to chest-deep water with your child in the Pass Hold (see p43). Throw a floating rubber toy or ball 90–120cm (3–4ft) ahead of you. Holding your child above the water, encourage him to go and get the toy and move him slowly towards it, praising any attempts he makes to kick. Once he catches the toy, praise him again.

SECOND OPTION

If your child isn't eager to chase a toy, he is likely to love this baby version of tag. Hold your child as for the first option, while your partner stands just ahead of you and encourages your child to "kick your feet and get me". Your partner should keep walking slightly ahead of you and your child until your child is allowed to catch him and get a hug as a reward.

ABOVE-WATER PASS

The simple action of passing your child to your partner above water builds trust and familiarity. This basic pass will be used and adapted throughout this chapter and eventually leads to your child accomplishing an unaided swim between his parents (see pp66–67). Establishing a common repeatable pattern helps your child assimilate new skills as he will recognize and be reassured by the familiar action of the above-water pass.

OBJECTIVES AND TIPS

To introduce different pass positions slowly, in a non-threatening, above-water situation.

To get your child used to being passed from one adult to another.

Practise this new skill during the Pick-a-ball Game (see p49) as you pass your child to your partner.

1 Play the Pick-a-ball Game (see p49) as part of the Activity Circuit (see pp52–53) and ask your child to select a favourite toy or ball. Stand in waist- to chest-deep water opposite the receiving partner, 60–90cm (2–3ft) apart. Hold your baby in the Pass Hold (see p43) and toss the toy across to the receiver. Encourage your child to get the toy, then move him forwards towards the receiver. Your baby may kick or he may simply glide with his head above the water.

2 The receiving partner should have his hands outstretched as your child approaches him, ready to catch and reward your child with the toy. After picking your child up and praising him, he should turn towards the bucket on the pool wall, encouraging your child to kick towards it and to put the toy in the bucket.

CHEEK DIP

Brushing your child's cheek gently across the surface of the water is a great way to expose him to the sensation of water sheeting across his face. After getting him used to the feeling of water on his head in the bath (see Bathtime Fun, pp38–39), you will now bring your child's face into close proximity to the pool water in preparation for his first submersion (see opposite).

TEACHING TIPS

Once your child is used to the Above-water Pass (see p57) as part of the Pick-a-ball Game, replace it with the Cheek Dip.

If you feel your child resisting in any way, stop, and try again after a few more lessons.

1 Stand in waist- to chest-deep water and hold your child in the Pass Hold (see p43). Lift him up 20–25cm (8–10in) so he is in an upright position with just his legs in the water. Start to bring him across the front of your body slowly.

2 As you bring him across your body, rotate your wrists so he is turned onto one side, and bring him down to the water. Gently lay the back of his head, ear and the edge of his cheek on the water. Continue your arm movement across your body and let his face brush along the water's surface. Then lift him and repeat the action the other way, gently brushing his opposite ear and cheek along the surface. Once he is comfortable with water on his cheek, brush the corner of his mouth along the water (to prepare for breath-holding skills).

CHEEK ROLL

Once your child is relaxed and comfortable practising the Cheek Dip (see opposite), he will be ready for his first true submersion, where his face is placed under the water briefly. If your baby becomes at all tense or frightened while doing this action, go back to the Water Pouring Station (see pp46–47) for more water adjustment.

TEACHING TIPS

Once your child is comfortable with the Cheek Dip (see p58) as part of the Pick-a-ball Game, replace it with the Cheek Roll.

If your child is three or older, practise Facial Submersions (see pp80–81) instead of this skill.

1 Stand in waist- to chest-deep water opposite a receiving partner, 90–120cm (3–4ft) apart. Hold your baby in the Pass Hold (see p43), then lift him up 20–25cm (8–10in) so that he is in an upright position with just his legs in the water. Turn your wrists and move him gently across your front, bringing him down towards the water so his cheek is in the water. To help keep the motion smooth for steps one and two, say it aloud: "lift, brush, roll, up".

2 As he moves across your front, roll your wrists so that his face turns to the surface of the water and his mouth and eyes briefly enter the water, then lift him up and out of the water into the receiver's hands. The receiver should re-direct your baby's attention with a toy or new activity, praise him and check quickly for any discomfort or coughing.

THE BREATH-HOLDING CUE

Once your baby enjoys having water poured over her head and face and is happy carrying out the Cheek Roll (see p59), it's time to teach her a new way to go under the water. The Breath-holding Cue is an important technique to learn, but should only be attempted when your instincts assure you that your child is ready.

TEACHING TIPS

Once your child is used to the Cheek Roll (see p59) as part of the Pick-a-ball Game, replace it with the Breath-holding Cue. At first, practise just half-second dips.

If your child is three or older, practise Facial Submersions (see pp80–81) instead of this skill.

1 Stand facing your partner in waist-deep water, 90–120cm (3–4ft) apart. The receiving parent should hold a toy in her hands above the water. Hold your child in the Pass Hold (see p43), then take two steps forwards while counting aloud "1, 2, 3". On "3", lift her 20–25cm (8–10in) up from the water, then lower her towards the water. The lifting and counting cues should have signalled to her that she will be going under water, but check that she is ready – her eyes should be closed but her mouth may be open. Carry on lowering her gently so she goes under water. (Note that as your child becomes more competent over the weeks, months and years, you can gradually decrease the height of the lift to 10cm (4in).)

2 Move your child forwards towards your partner, with her face just below the surface of the water, taking another step if necessary.

3 After half a second, bring your child up above the surface of the water into the hands of the receiver. The receiver should check your child for any coughing, but more importantly, praise her and divert her attention. Don't worry if she looks surprised, but if she cries, move on to a different activity. Repeat a maximum of three times each lesson in different rounds of the Activity Circuit (see pp52–53).

FACE-TO-FACE DIP

In this alternative method of submersion, you dip your child under water while she is facing towards you, so she will see your happy, approving face as she comes out of the dip and is reassured if this technique startles her. Use the count and lift of the Breath-holding Cue (see pp60–61) to get your child ready to go under water, submerging her for between half a second and three seconds depending on her ability and level of comfort.

TEACHING TIPS

Standing in chest-deep water will help you to hold your child's weight comfortably, even though your arms are extended.

Walk backwards at an even and smooth pace throughout.

Check that your baby's body is stretching out behind her with her feet up near the surface.

1 Stand in chest-deep water with your child in the Face-to-face Hold (see p43). Extend your arms out, with your elbows slightly bent, to make a space between you and your child. Walk slowly backwards and count "1, 2, 3". On "3", lift your child 10–30cm (4–10in) above the water. Her eyes should close in response to the lift cue.

2 Continue walking backwards slowly as you bring your child down from the lift and submerge her face just under the surface of the water. Bring her up again after half to one second, then distract her with a toy. As you practise over time, you can gradually increase the time submerged to three seconds.

JUMP FROM THE WALL

Learning a safe way to jump from the pool wall into the water ensures that your child clears the hard concrete surfaces of the wall and lands safely in the water or in your arms. At first, she will be fully guided by you to jump. Then, as time progresses, she will begin initiating her own lean towards you after you have given her a touch cue (moving your hands under her armpits), and will jump on her own after you have cued her verbally.

FIRST LEVEL

1 Stand in waist- to chest-deep water and place your child in a sitting position on the pool wall with your hands under her armpits. While you steady her, count aloud "1, 2, 3". On "3", gently move your hands forwards in a rubbing motion under your child's armpits to cue her to jump. Keep your hands under her armpits as she jumps to you, but do not pull her hands or wrists to force a jump.

2 As she bends at the waist, allow her to come forwards in a jump so that her bottom leaves the wall last. Catch her before her head goes under the water.

SECOND LEVEL

Once your child is comfortable at the first level, cue her as before, but when she leans forwards, keep your hands slightly away from her body and catch her in your open hands as her face splashes the surface of the water.

FIRST HELD UNDERWATER SWIM

Once your child is comfortable with brief frontal submersions, is competent at practising the Breath-holding Cue (see pp60–61), and comes out of her dip happy and holding her breath consistently, you are ready to try the First Held Underwater Swim. This stage will build up your child's endurance, transforming a brief half-second dip into first a one-, then two-, and finally a three-second held submersion with successful breath holding.

FIRST LEVEL

TEACHING TIPS

Once your child is comfortable with the Breath-holding Cue (see pp60–61) as part of the Pick-a-ball Game, replace it with the First Held Underwater Swim.

If your child is three or older, practise this swim but adapt it so that your child self-submerges after being given a verbal cue (see p82), then move on to the First Short Swim (see pp82–83).

1 Stand in waist- to chest-deep water holding your baby in the Pass Hold (see p43). You should be facing your partner, about 1.2–1.5m (4–5ft) apart. Give your child the Breath-holding Cue (see pp60–61), then move your baby down towards the water.

2 As your child's face is submerged, both you and the receiver should slowly count, "1, 2" as you walk forwards slowly, keeping your baby's face just below the water's surface. On "2", lift her out of the water to the receiver, who should check quickly that she hasn't swallowed any water, before praising her and re-directing her attention with a toy. Repeat three times each lesson, spread out at intervals during the lesson, in different rounds of the Activity Circuit (see pp52–53), for at least four lessons before moving on to the second level.

SECOND LEVEL
Once your child accomplishes the first level comfortably, you can increase the time she is held and guided underwater gradually, by an additional second. Follow as for the first level, but slowly count "1, 2, 3" aloud before you lift her out to the receiver. Practise three times each lesson, again spread out at intervals during the lesson in different rounds of the Activity Circuit.

FIRST UNAIDED UNDERWATER SWIM

Weeks of play, practice and patience are about to culminate in an amazing event... a brief, unaided swim. For the first time, a child will feel weightless in the water as he swims between his parents, experiencing the joy and freedom of movement. This new, flowing motion stimulates growth on many levels – lung capacity will gradually increase, as will motor skills and spatial awareness.

TEACHING TIPS

Once your child is comfortable with the First Held Underwater Swim (pp64–65) as part of the Pick-a-ball Game, replace it with the First Unaided Underwater Swim.

If your child is three or older, practise the First Short Swim (see pp82–83) instead of this skill.

Ensure you are calm but upbeat.

1 Stand facing your partner in waist- to chest-deep water, 1.2m (4ft) apart. Hold your child in the Pass Hold (see p43), then give him the Breath-holding Cue (see pp60–61). Check that he is holding his breath, then move forwards slowly, submerging him so his face is under water. Release him below the surface, pushing him forwards gently.

2 With the receiver, slowly count aloud "1, 2", from the moment of submersion. Always ensure that the amount of time for which your child is submerged never exceeds his current readiness. Your child should be in a horizontal position and may be kicking or gliding.

3 On the count of "2", the receiver should gently place his hands under your child's armpits and lift him out above the water. The receiver should quickly check your child is comfortable, then praise him and redirect his attention with a toy or new activity. This first swim will be just two seconds long, and you should limit the number of swims per lesson to between three and five. Increase the length of this swim by one second every three to 10 lessons depending on your child's readiness and comfort, until your child can swim unaided for five seconds.

BALANCE

Finding balance in the water is a unique feeling and complements learning to balance on land. For a baby in the water, the dense liquid environment with its altered gravity envelops him, supports him and buoys him as he learns to find and maintain his centre of gravity. "Riding" a noodle is a good way to teach your child to balance as he will need to adjust to a bobbing surface beneath him repeatedly, whilst moving forwards, changing direction or going round in circles.

SAFETY TIPS

Babies are quick movers, so be ready to steady rapid movements that may cause a loss of balance.

When your baby is sitting on or in a floating object, always keep your hands on him or stay within hand's reach of him.

Remember that floating pool toys are not lifesaving devices, so never leave your child alone in the pool.

1 Place your child on the middle of a noodle, so that he is straddling it and riding it like a horse. You can either hold him from the side or sit behind him and hold him round his waist.

2 Sing a horse-related song such as "She'll be Comin' Round the Mountain". For the first verse walk your child round in a circle to the left; for the second verse switch and circle to the right. Follow by slowly spinning your child round 360° twice to the left, then twice to the right. End with three big jumps in place.

TIME TO GO

Even if your child is tired, she may not want to leave the pool, especially if she's had fun. An exit ritual signals that it's time to go, which can make the transition smoother. At the end of each lesson we sing "Ring-a-ring of Rosies". For several weeks, merely sprinkle water over your child's head during the last verse. Weeks later, when your child has fully mastered the Breath-holding Cue (see pp60–61) and can perform an unaided swim (see pp66–67), she can go under the water vertically at the end of the song.

(see pp60–61) ... (see pp66–67)

TEACHING TIPS

Lift your baby up smoothly, lower down smoothly and lift smoothly back up again as if in one long connected movement.

If your child is happy being submerged and you would like to submerge with her, hold her so that she is facing you, lift her, then audibly take a breath and briefly submerge together.

1 In waist- to chest-deep water, hold your child under her armpits, facing away from you. Sing the nursery rhyme "Ring-a-ring of Rosies" and walk round in a circle to the left. When you sing "We all fall...", stand still, then lift your child up vertically 25–30cm (10–12in).

2 As you sing "...down", lower her under the water smoothly, covering her head for about half to one second. (For several weeks, when your child is just a beginner, simply drizzle water over her head instead of submerging her.)

3 After the brief dip, smoothly lift her up above the surface of the water, then turn her around to face you and praise her for doing so well in the lesson. She will soon come to realize that this action signifies the end of the lesson, and that it is now time to leave the pool.

BEGINNERS: STAGE TWO
(MINIMUM AGE ONE YEAR)

STAGE TWO LESSON PLAN

REQUIREMENTS FOR STAGE TWO

Minimum Age: Your child should be at least one year old.

Skill Level: Your child has successfully completed all the techniques in stage one (pp54–69). He has acquired water-adjustment skills, has learned the Breath-holding Cue, can jump from the wall into your arms and can move through the water in a brief, unaided swim.

As your child develops from a baby into a toddler, he becomes more active and playful in the pool. During this part of the programme he strengthens all the foundation skills he has acquired in stage one, but now you can add new activities such as Kicking Drills (see p72) and Monkey Walk (see p77), which will suit his increased abilities.

As before, work through the exercises in this section in the order in which they appear and introduce the skills based on your child's readiness and comfort. Children who are relaxed, receptive and happy in the water may progress very quickly through the skills, whilst hesitant or cautious children will need to spend more time during each lesson simply playing and at the Water Pouring Station (see pp46–47). Don't rush and you will find that over the weeks and months your child learns new skills at his own pace.

For toddlers expressing their independence, do not make the pool or the lesson a battleground. Allowing choice at the Water Pouring Station and during the Pick-a-ball Game (see p49) gives your child some control over his environment. The playful structure of the lesson plan also keeps your child engaged in the pool. As always, adapt the plan to suit the pool you are in.

LESSON PLAN

WARM UP 3–5 minutes
Practise kicking and chasing a toy or kicking drills.   *pp56; 72*

SONG BREAK 3–5 minutes
Sing "The Wheels on the Bus" or a bathtime song.
Incorporate bubble blowing into the song.   *pp39; 73*

ACTIVITY CIRCUIT 10–12 minutes total   *pp52–53*
Structure the circuit as shown below. Go round the circuit 3–5 times per lesson, spending a short time at each "station" before you move on to the next.
a) **Water Pouring Station**   *pp46–47*
b) **Monkey Walk**   *p77*
c) **Jump from the Wall** (once per round)   *p63*
d) **Pick-a-ball Game**   *p49*
    By this stage your child should have learned the submersion skills for stage one gradually and sequentially. Continue to submerge your child during the game using the technique for the First Unaided Underwater Swim (see pp66–67), but do not repeat this more than 3–5 times per lesson. Use the Above-water Pass (see p57) instead to give your child a rest from being submerged.
e) **Basketball**   *p45*

SONG or GAME BREAK 2–4 minutes
Sing or play one or two songs or games.   *pp48–51*

WALL APPROACHES AND JUMPS 5 minutes total
Pool Wall Approaches
Reaching for and Grabbing the Wall (first or second level depending on ability) 3–4 times max   *p74*
Jumps from the Wall
Jump from the Wall (first or second level depending on ability) 3–4 times max   *p63*

BALANCE 3–5 minutes   *p68*

TIME TO GO 1 minute   *p69*

KICKING DRILLS

As your child develops and starts to walk and even run, he will bring increased coordination to bear on his kick – and the splashes will get bigger, too. Although some new beginners may not kick and will simply glide for a while, children in this age group generally exhibit a more pronounced learned kick. Eventually, with practice, a steady up-and-down kick (a "flutter") can be achieved, so try these kicking drills with him.

TEACHING TIPS

Encourage your child to watch and then imitate other children and adults as they kick in the water, as he will be motivated by the resulting splashes.

Teach your child to associate the verbal command "kick, kick" with a specific physical activity to be performed by him.

OPTION FOR YOUNGER CHILDREN

In chest-deep water, stand with your child held facing away from you and directly in front of you in a simulated sitting position in the water. Your partner should kick vigorously in front of both of you. Say the words "kick, kick" and point to your partner's splashing feet. Then encourage your child to repeat what they have seen: "make big splashes and get us all wet!"

OPTION FOR OLDER CHILDREN

Sit side-by-side on the pool wall, with your feet in the water. If your child is nervous, he can start off sitting on your lap. Demonstrate a kick for your child, repeating the words "kick, kick, kick" as you perform the movement, then ask your child to kick with you.

BLOWING BUBBLES

Bubble blowing before the age of five helps children get used to touching the surface of the water with their lips. It is not required for submersion and swimming, but it does help with learning breath control and breath holding. This is a good age to introduce bubble blowing as older babies and toddlers are increasingly aware of your mouth movements and will attempt to mimic the sounds you make.

TEACHING TIPS

Make sure your child's face is close enough to the water so she can bend forwards and reach it, but never push her lips towards the water to make her try.

A little coughing or spluttering may occur at first. This will stop once your child can produce a steady outwards flow of air.

FIRST OPTION

Hold your child in the Face-to-face or Pass Hold (see p43). She should be close enough to the water so she can tip her face forwards and touch it. First, blow air above the water, then put your mouth in the water and blow bubbles. Let her watch you so she can copy you, then encourage her to blow bubbles with you.

SECOND OPTION

If your child is worried about blowing bubbles directly into the pool water, either blow bubbles in your cupped hand filled with water or use a shallow plastic bowl. Again, let your child watch you blowing bubbles, then encourage her to copy you.

REACHING FOR AND GRABBING THE WALL

Learning to reach for and grab the stability of the pool wall sets an early desirable pattern for safety skills learned later in the programme. The skills of reaching and grabbing acquired in these two exercises will ultimately develop into the more sophisticated skills of turning around and grabbing the wall for safety, as well as shimmying along the wall or climbing the wall to exit the pool.

OBJECTIVES

To learn to reach out ahead and grab the pool wall with the head above the water.

To accomplish a sturdy grip on the wall while being held.

To hold the wall unaided successfully for five seconds.

To reach for and grab the wall after a cued, held submersion.

FIRST LEVEL

1 Place a toy on the pool wall or in the gutter. With your child in the Pass Hold (see p43), stand back 1.5–1.8m (5–6ft) from the wall. Slowly approach the wall, encouraging your child to kick. When you are 25–30cm (10–12in) from the wall, stop. Ask your child to reach out and grab the wall.

2 Continue holding your child under the armpits and reward him with the toy when he grabs the wall. Gradually, after several practices, when your child is holding the wall firmly, begin slipping first one hand, then the other, away until your child is holding the wall by himself for five seconds.

SECOND LEVEL

Once your child can complete the first level successfully, and can carry out the Breath-holding Cue (see pp60–61) and First Unaided Underwater Swim (see pp66–67) confidently, you can submerge her as you approach the wall.

1 Place a toy on the wall. With your child in the Pass Hold (see p43), stand 1.5–1.8m (5–6ft) from the wall. Give her the Breath-holding Cue and check she is ready to go under water. Submerge her briefly and propel her towards the wall, then return her to the surface 30cm (1ft) before the wall.

2 Keeping your hands under your child's armpits, ask her to grab the wall. Approach the wall slowly so that she will not bump her head on the concrete. Praise her and give her the toy when she grabs the wall.

LEARNING TO WAIT

Teaching your child to wait for a cue from an adult before entering a body of water is a vital safety skill. Along with the safe pool entries (see pp41–42) and sitting jumps from the wall (see p63), learning to wait is an important skill for your child to learn, both in and out of the pool.

OBJECTIVES AND TIPS

To establish important safety rules from an early age and teach your child to enter the pool only with your permission.

Use this technique every time you practise jumping from the wall.

FIRST OPTION

Standing in waist-deep water, place your child on the wall so he is ready for a jump. If he begins to lean or jump prematurely, put your right hand flat on his chest and your left hand under his right armpit. Tell him to "wait until I have counted to 3". Count to cue the jump, keeping your hands in the same position while you count "1, 2". As you reach "3", move your right hand to under his left armpit, cueing him to jump. Catch him as per the instructions for jumping from the wall (see p63).

SECOND OPTION

Once a child is walking and running on her own, enforcing safety rules will keep her away from immediate danger. Before entering the pool area with your child, hold her hand and tell her to walk with you. If she begins to run towards the pool by herself, firmly call to her to "wait". Walk up to her quickly, hold her hand and tell her, "Do not go in unless I am with you." Do not discipline your child, but firmly tell her she must not go in on her own.

MONKEY WALK

Rob imagined a small monkey edging along a branch when he named this hand-by-hand shimmy. This drill is a vital part of early safety skills as it teaches a child to move safely in the pool alone, even if he can't swim. Once a child can grab the wall, he can shimmy over to the nearest ladder or steps and exit the pool.

TEACHING TIPS

Place a toy 1.2m (4ft) away from your child in the gutter. Reward him with the toy once he has reached it by himself.

Practise as part of the Activity Circuit (see pp52–53).

FIRST LEVEL

Position your child so that he is gripping the pool gutter or wall firmly, and place a toy in the gutter or on the wall 1.2m (4ft) away from you. Stand behind him with your hands on top of his. Slide his right hand along the gutter, then slide his left hand towards his right hand so they meet. As you move his hands say aloud "slide… together". Repeat this action as you move along the wall until your child reaches the toy.

SECOND LEVEL

Once your child has learned how to monkey walk with your hands guiding hers, she can try it on her own. Stand alongside your child, about 30–60cm (1–2ft) in front of her, with both of you gripping the gutter. Encourage her to chase you as you monkey walk ahead of her. Once she catches you, give her a big hug.

ADAPTATIONS FOR THREE- TO FOUR-YEAR-OLD BEGINNERS

ADAPTED LESSON PLAN

REQUIREMENTS FOR STAGE THREE

Minimum Age: Your child should be at least three years old.

Skill Level: Your child is a beginner. You should have played at home in the bath already, so he is accustomed to the feel of water (see Bathtime Fun, pp38–39), and visited and played in the pool to help him adjust to the new environment (see First Trip to the Pool, pp40–43).

This section is specifically adapted for beginners over the age of three. Unlike younger counterparts, they should be full participants in the "when" and "how" of submersions, practising self-submersions rather than being submerged by their parent. To address the needs of the eager, as well as the frightened, beginner, we have included a number of games that allow your child to practise self-submersion, so he learns to put his face in the water willingly.

Follow the lesson plan here to guide you through the techniques in Stage One and this section, which substitutes self-initiated submersions for parent-initiated ones. Note that you should only practise the First Held Underwater Swim (see pp64–65) or First Short Swim (see pp82–83) once your child can self-submerge confidently at the pool steps (see pp80–81), then when held in the open water. To adapt pp80–81 for open water (for a facial self-submersion during the pass in Pick-a-ball Game) the sending parent holds the child opposite the receiving parent, 30–46cm (12–18in) away. Use techniques from levels 1, 3 or 4, encouraging your child to dip his own face briefly in the water, then transfer him to the receiving parent who praises him and re-directs his attention to finish the game.

Once your child has mastered the skills in this stage, move on to Stage Two, again substituting self-initiated submersions for parent-initiated ones.

LESSON PLAN

WARM UP 3 minutes
Practise kicking and chasing a toy or kicking drills.   *pp56; 72*

SONG BREAK 3–5 minutes
Sing "The Wheels on the Bus" or a bathtime song.   *p39*

ACTIVITY CIRCUIT 10–12 minutes total   *pp52–53*
Structure the circuit as shown below. Go round 3–5 times.
a) **Water Pouring Station**   *pp46–47*
b) **Monkey Walk**   *p77*
c) **Pick-a-ball Game** (at appropriate level – see below)   *p49*
   This game involves passing your child between parents while introducing submersion skills. As your child adjusts to one skill, move on to the next in the order given. Use the Above-water Pass for some circuits so your child isn't submerged too often. Only practise the swims once your child happily self-submerges.
   i) Above-water Pass   *p57*
   ii) Cheek Dip 3–5 times max   *p58*
   iii) Facial self-submersion (adapted for open water) see *left*
   iv) First Held Underwater Swim with self-submersion (see p82) 2–4 times max   *pp64–65*
   v) First Short Swim 3–4 times max   *pp82–83*
d) **Basketball**   *p45*
e) **Facial Submersions** 2–4 times max   *pp80–81*
f) **Alligator Walk**   *p85*
g) **Standing Step Jump** or **Jump from the Wall**   *pp84; 63*

SONG or GAME BREAK 2–4 minutes   *pp48–51*

WALL APPROACHES AND JUMPS 5 minutes total
a) **Reaching for and Grabbing the Wall** (first level, or second level with self-submersion, depending on ability) 3 times max   *p74*
b) **Jump from the Wall** (first or second level depending on ability) 3–4 times max   *p63*

BALANCE 3–5 minutes   *p68*

TIME TO GO 1 minute   *p69*

FACIAL SUBMERSIONS

You need to approach the technique of facial submersion for three- to four-year-olds in a different way than for younger children. At these ages, children become full participants in the "when" and "how" of submerging their faces in the water. By using playful games, your child will initiate this defining moment and submerge her face herself. Her face will beam with pride and a sense of accomplishment in conquering the unknown.

TEACHING TIPS

Never force your child's head under the water.

Self-initiated submersion may come excitedly the first day or it may take weeks of practice – your child may also put her face in the water one day and not want to the next. Don't worry about these hiccups – go at your child's pace.

FIRST LEVEL

With your child sitting on a shallow pool step if she is nervous, hold her in the Face-to-face Hold (see p43) with your arms outstretched and your elbows slightly bent. Play a game of "quick draw" – who can dip their face in and out of the water fastest. Start by dipping your eyes, nose and mouth in and out of the water, then ask her to copy you and see if she can do it as quickly as you.

SECOND LEVEL

Stand in chest-deep water with your hands gripping the pool wall. Ask your child to hold on to the wall next to you. Tell her that you are going to play a game of Peek A Boo. Pop your head under the water, then come up and quickly say "Peek A Boo. Your turn!" You may need to go up and down two or three times before she copies you, and at first she may just dip her chin in the water and not her whole face.

THIRD LEVEL

Sit facing your child on a shallow pool step. Take your finger and pretend to "paint" the colours of the rainbow one at a time on your child's forehead. Ask her to tell you which colour comes next. Now ask her to "wash off" the imaginary paint and encourage her to lean forwards and dip all or part of her face into the water. Repeat a few times.

FOURTH LEVEL

Hide some colourful "treasure" on a shallow pool step, such as plastic weighted toys, coins, costume jewellery or dive rings. With both you and your child wearing goggles, put your face in the water first to look at the sunken objects. Then encourage your child to come and dip her face in and look at the treasure with you.

FIRST SHORT SWIM

Your child's first unaided swim is the culmination of months of practice – this is one of life's big moments! Before you try this technique, ensure your child self-submerges confidently as shown on pp80–81. Next, practise both levels of the First Held Underwater Swim (see pp64–65), but with your child choosing to submerge his own face in the water by allowing you to count him in instead of being given a lift cue. This means that, before he learns the First Short Swim, he will be able to hold his breath and go under water without needing you to initiate the submersion.

OBJECTIVES

To provide a secure, trustworthy base from which – and towards which – your child can swim.

To maintain and increase your child's confidence in the water. His self-esteem will grow as he realizes he doesn't need you to give him a cue for submersion.

To help your child to hold his breath, self-submerge and swim unaided for two seconds.

1 Standing in chest-deep water and facing your partner, about 60–90cm (2–3ft) apart, hold your child in the Pass Hold (see p43). Ask your child to stretch out his hands towards your partner, with his palms facing downwards. Tell him, "When you put your face in, I'm going to send you over to [the receiver]. Keep your face in until you touch her hands, then come up and say 'hello'" Reach your child towards the receiver's outstretched hands (her palms should be facing upwards) and let him touch them to show him how close her hands are.

2 Ask your child if he is ready to go under water, then as he holds his breath and submerges, push him slightly forwards and release your hands from under his armpits. As he is submerged, count "1, 2". The receiver lets your child reach out and touch her hands, then catches your child's hands in hers. Your child should either lift his own head up and say "hello" to the receiver after this two-second swim, or be lifted up. Praise your child.

STANDING STEP JUMP

There is often a wonderful exuberance when children jump into the water, and they love to repeat this activity again and again. Where you get your child to perform this jump is important. If you position her in waist- to chest-deep water, her face is already close to the surface and she need only lean forwards to reach you. While some children will quickly turn this small jump into a leap, others will need time before they even lean towards you.

1 Help your child to stand on a pool step so that she is in waist- to chest-deep water. Stand directly in front of her on the pool floor. Ask her to stand on the edge of the step and curl her toes over the edge. Brushing your hands under her armpits, count "1, 2, 3", then encourage her to bend her knees, lean over, push herself off the step and jump forwards towards you. Keep your hands close to her as she jumps towards you, and catch her while her face is still above the water.

2 Now, help her to get up to the top step. Guide her to stand on the bottom step, or the middle step if the bottom step is too deep. Position her so she is facing away from you and towards the steps. Ask her to put her arms out and, on your count of "1, 2, 3", lean towards the top step and reach for it with her hands. Once she has her hands firmly on the top step she can climb up the steps. Stand behind her so that you can help her if she needs it.

ALLIGATOR WALK

This fun exercise was inspired by alligators stretching out flat while sunning themselves in shallow water. In this game, you ask your child to lie on the shallow steps of the pool and act like an alligator. The position allows him to experience the correct horizontal body alignment for swimming and to extend his legs. Plus, he will become used to having his face near the water, which helps him to become even more accustomed to submersions.

OBJECTIVES AND TIPS

To help promote a good, flat, elongated body position and an up-and-down kick.

If you want to get your child used to having his face in the water, ask him to blow bubbles as well.

Practise as part of the Activity Circuit (see pp52–53).

FIRST LEVEL

Help your child to lie flat on his stomach at one end of the shallow pool step. Stand at the other end of the step and ask him to crawl towards you on his stomach, using his arms to pull himself forwards. Now ask him to also kick his feet. The step should stop his knees from bending fully, which will help to promote a more efficient kick.

SECOND LEVEL

Once your child is comfortable with the first level, you can ask him to blow bubbles or make alligator-like grunts and growls as he kicks and moves along the pool step. All of these activities will help him to get used to the feel of water on his face, and will make this exercise seem more like a fun game. Eventually, he will be happy to put his entire face in the water.

SWIMMING UNAIDED

Congratulations! Your child can now submerge on cue successfully, swim comfortably for five seconds while holding her breath, kick steadily, propel herself forwards confidently, and emerge from her swim happily without having swallowed any water. As a learning team, you and your child are now ready to add new, more complex skills to your repertoire, such as turning around under water, floating and diving for rings. As always, our goal in this chapter is a relaxed, happy child who is enjoying the process of learning to swim. Progressing at your child's pace, and making each lesson playful and fun will result in a child who is truly at home in the water.

TEACHING INTERMEDIATES

This chapter is designed for parents and children who have achieved the basic water confidence skills and are ready for more complex techniques. It should only be started once your child can perform the skills in the Water Confidence chapter competently and happily.

There is no big jump from beginners to intermediates. Instead, it is part of a gradual process that builds on all the skills that your child has learned in the previous chapter, so that he is not only able to swim, but truly loves the water. This chapter is divided into three stages, each with a minimum age requirement. Make sure you don't teach a child any skills that are meant for older children. Instead, stick to the skills for your child's age group so you introduce them at the optimal time, when age, ability and readiness all intersect.

Remember that you should progress only when your child is comfortable, practise consistently in enjoyable lessons and avoid frustration by practising complex activities only for short intervals and at times when your child's energy levels are highest.

Water Pouring Station and Activity Circuit

As for beginners, the Water Pouring Station (see pp46–47) and Activity Circuit (see pp52–53) are still key parts of the learning process. But whereas with beginners most of the Activity Circuit was carried out in their parent's arms or on top of the water, now your child may carry out some of the exercises with his face in the water, and with less assistance.

Games and songs

These still play a very important role in teaching your child at the intermediate levels, and group games become more valuable as your child learns to copy and imitate his peers. This helps him to overcome his fears as he will watch other children performing the actions he is nervous about. He will also learn to share toys or your attention with others.

Lesson plan

Use the suggested lesson plans given at the start of each intermediates stage as the basis of your 30-minute lessons, but amend them to suit your child's readiness, experience, abilities and skill level. The basic structure of the lesson should remain relatively similar, but as your child learns more skills, they can be absorbed into the regular structure of your lessons. Try and have at least two, and ideally four, lessons per week, as this continuity will help your child learn quickly and retain skills – long breaks may require periods of re-learning.

Your child may pick up certain skills very quickly, while others may take weeks or months of practice. Go at your child's pace and don't push him to learn.

To keep your child interested in the lesson and to practise all the skills he has learned, limit the time spent on any one activity to seven minutes or less. Make sure you enjoy the lesson and do not rush, but remember that a young child's attention span may be best suited to changing intervals of play.

INTERMEDIATES: STAGE ONE (pp90–101)

You can start Intermediates: Stage One if your child is at least 14 months old and has mastered all the age-appropriate skills in the Water Confidence chapter. Let feedback from your child guide you as you introduce new skills, modify old ones and help him increase his proficiency in the water.

INTERMEDIATES: STAGE TWO (pp102–09)

Once your child is at least 19 months old, has completed all the age-appropriate skills in the Water Confidence chapter, and can carry out all the skills in Intermediates: Stage One competently, move on to Intermediates: Stage Two.

Now that your child has reached a period of increased coordination in his physical and mental development, and can swim comfortably for seven seconds with a strong, steady kick, as well as hold his breath and enjoy it, he can add an important safety sequence to his swimming abilities. Although The Safety Sequence (see pp108–09) does not make your child "drownproof", it will enable him to swim to safety should he ever fall into a pool.

INTERMEDIATES: STAGE THREE (pp110–23)

When your child has mastered all the age-appropriate skills in the Water Confidence chapter, has completed Intermediates: Stages One and Two, and is at least three years old, progress to Intermediates: Stage Three.

Experienced swimmers of this age are strong and capable and manoeuvre further and faster in the pool than younger children. They can swim a distance of 6m (20 feet), and are truly at home in the water. During this stage an important step is conquered when your child learns to surface for a breath (see pp112–15) independently.

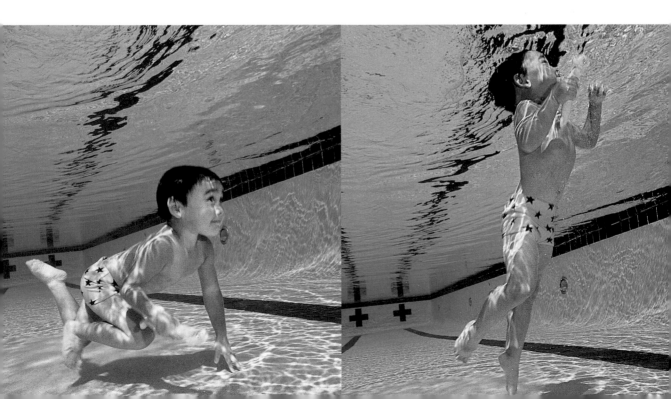

INTERMEDIATES: STAGE ONE
(MINIMUM AGE 14 MONTHS)

STAGE ONE LESSON PLAN

REQUIREMENTS FOR STAGE ONE

Minimum Age: Your child should be at least 14 months old.

Skill Level: Your child has successfully completed Beginners: Stages One and Two, as well as the Adaptations for Three- to Four-year-old Beginners if she started learning to swim over the age of 36 months. She can propel herself comfortably with a steady kick, face submerged, holding her breath for five seconds without taking in water.

For the first of the intermediate stages, the lesson plan is now adapted slightly to allow for the addition of more complex skills. These include Rob's Tai Chi Pass (see pp92–93), which encourages an efficient swimming posture and kick, as well as Turning Around Under Water (see pp100–01), which begins to introduce the individual skills needed to accomplish The Safety Sequence later (see pp108–09).

Because the lesson plan for intermediates is simply an extension of those for beginners, your sessions will feel very familiar to your child. This helps create a smooth transition from the foundation skills to these more complex skills. You will also find that your child's endurance and proficiency will be increasing.

As before, use the lesson plan as a guideline only, and plan your lessons according to your child's readiness, comfort and current abilities.

Note that younger children will still need to be given the Breath-holding Cue (see pp60–61) before being submerged under water by their parent. However, children over the age of three can simply be given a verbal cue rather than the lift cue involved in the Breath-holding Cue.

LESSON PLAN

WARM UP 3–5 minutes
Practise kicking and chasing a toy or
kicking drills.   *pp56; 72*

SONG BREAK 3–5 minutes
Sing "The Wheels on the Bus" or a bathtime song.   *p39*

WARM-UP DIPS 1–2 minutes
Short, cued dips using the techniques for
First Held Underwater Swim.   *pp64–65*

ACTIVITY CIRCUIT 10–12 minutes total   *pp52–53*
Structure the circuit as shown below. Go round
the circuit 3–5 times per lesson, spending a
short time at each "station" before moving on
to the next.
a) **Water Pouring Station**   *pp46–47*
b) **Monkey Walk or Basketball**   *pp77; 45*
c) **Jump from the Wall** (second level)   *p63*
d) **Pick-a-ball Game**   *p49*
   For the pass between parents introduce the skills
   below gradually, and in the order given.
   i) Rob's Tai Chi Pass 3–5 times max   *pp92–93*
   ii) Fin Fun 3–5 times max   *pp94–95*

APPROACHING THE WALL 3–5 minutes total
Guided Swim to the Wall (first or second level
depending on ability) 3 times max   *pp96–97*

JUMP OFF THE WALL 3–5 minutes total
Jump, Dip and Swim (first or second level
depending on ability) 3 times max   *pp98–99*

BALANCE or RUN AND JUMP
3–5 minutes   *pp68; 51*

TIME TO GO 1 minute   *p69*
Turning Around Under Water (first or second
level depending on ability) 1–2 times max   *pp100–101*

ROB'S TAI CHI PASS

To provide a boost to swimmers who are ready to increase the distance and duration of their swim, Rob devised a special Tai Chi-like pass for parents to use. This pass not only provides forwards momentum towards a receiving parent, it also balances, aligns and positions the body in an efficient, prone, horizontal position and stimulates your child to kick.

TEACHING TIPS

The forwards movement is generated at the shin or foot area, not at the head. You should merely guide the head with your fingertips and not push forwards.

"Flick" the foot lightly at the end of the sequence to stimulate the kick.

2 Once your fingers touch his neck, slip your non-dominant hand out from under your child's other armpit and brush it down along the side of his body. At this point your dominant hand should still be in contact with your child's head, guiding it forwards, while your non-dominant hand should be in contact with his torso (as your child becomes more proficient you can let go with this hand). Balance him if he needs it.

1 Stand in waist- to chest-deep water opposite your partner, 1.2–1.5m (4–5ft) apart. Hold your child in the Pass Hold (see p43) and cue him to go under water. As his face enters the water, push forwards under both his armpits. The receiver should count the number of seconds for which your child is submerged, ensuring that it does not exceed his current ability. Reposition your dominant hand (your right hand if you are right-handed) at the base of his head by slipping your hand out from under his armpit, lifting your elbow and rotating your wrist so you place your fingertips at the base of his neck. Use your fingers to guide (but not push) the head forwards as he kicks.

3 Continue running your non-dominant hand along the side of your child's body until you reach either his shin, ankle or foot, depending on where the swing of his kick is. Flick the foot upwards and forwards lightly, so you push your child forwards slightly, stimulating a kick. At the moment of thrust, release your hands from your child's head and foot.

4 Both your hands should now be clear of your child, and he should be propelling himself forwards towards the receiver, who should catch him, lift him up out of the water and praise him.

FIN FUN

This is an ideal stage to introduce fins (flippers) to your child's lessons. They are good learning aids because they lift the foot to the top of the water (producing an efficient kick), and build and tone the leg muscles. However, ensure you practise without fins at times so you and your child are familiar with her natural abilities. Swimming at the surface through a hoop provides focus and motivation and encourages a streamlined body position.

OBJECTIVES AND TIPS

To improve kicking, body alignment and lung capability.

Allow your child time to adjust to the fins during kicking exercises.

If your child is unsure of the fins, practise wearing them in the bath.

Fins should be made of flexible rubber or soft plastic.

1 You will need three adults to practise hoop swims. The sender places fins on the child while she is sitting on the pool wall. Two adults stand opposite each other in waist- to chest-deep water, 1.2–1.8m (4–6ft) apart. The receiver should hold a dive ring or toy under the water to direct the child's eyes and head downwards. The third adult stands halfway between the sender and receiver, holding a hoop in the water. The sender should hold the child in the Pass Hold (see p43), encouraging her to "swim through the hoop to get the ring".

2 The sender should cue your child to go under water, then use Rob's Tai Chi Pass (see pp92–93) to guide her forwards through the hoop to the receiver. The child may grab the dive ring from the receiver. The sender should check that the number of seconds the child spends under water does not exceed her current ability. The receiver should catch the child and lift her out of the water. Increase the length of the swim gradually in one-second increments over the weeks and months.

GUIDED SWIM TO THE WALL

Your child has experienced the liberating sensation of an unaided swim between her parents. Swimming unaided to the wall occurs in very distinct stages, and to ensure your child has the correct body alignment and isn't alarmed by swimming towards a looming concrete wall, you need to guide her, first by holding her under the armpits, then with a reassuring touch at the back of the head.

OBJECTIVES

To encourage independent swimming towards the wall.

To maintain body alignment by providing hands-on guidance.

To link swimming to the wall with grabbing the wall.

To ensure your child is not alarmed by the looming sight of the pool wall when they open their eyes.

FIRST LEVEL

Place a toy on the wall as a target. With your child in the Pass Hold (see p43), stand 1.5–1.8m (5–6ft) from the wall. Your count will be "1, 2, lift, down, 1, 2, 3, grab the wall". Cue your child to go under water and submerge her (1, 2, lift, down). With both hands under her armpits walk slowly towards the wall as you count "1, 2, 3". Once you reach the wall, if your child does not automatically grab it and lift her head, lift her and tell her to "grab the wall". Reward her with the toy. You can gradually increase the length of time under water to match that of her unaided swim.

SECOND LEVEL

1 Once your child is comfortable at the first level, you can move on to the second level. Follow the first level, but stand 1.8m (6ft) from the wall. Your new count will be "1, 2, lift, down, high elbow, kick, kick, grab the wall". Cue your child to go under water and submerge her. As her face submerges, slip your dominant hand (your right hand if you are right-handed) out from under her armpit, raise your elbow and rotate your wrist so that your fingertips move from her armpit, over her back and end up behind her head at the base of her neck, guiding her towards the wall.

2 Continue guiding your child towards the wall for a count of two ("kick, kick") with your non-dominant hand firmly under your child's armpit. When she reaches the wall, she may reach out and grab it, but if she doesn't, use your non-dominant hand to lift her under her armpit and raise her to the surface asking her to "grab the wall". When she has grabbed the wall, praise and reward her with the toy.

JUMP, DIP AND SWIM

Your child has already learned how to carry out a safe, leaning jump from the wall (see p63), and now you can transform this skill into a jump, submersion and swim. At first, allow her only to submerge briefly while you guide her towards you under the water. Then, with time and practice, she will be able to accomplish a jump, dip and unaided swim under water towards you.

(see p63)

OBJECTIVES AND TIPS

To maintain the correct forwards-lean position when jumping.

If your child hesitates when jumping, move closer to her and keep your hands on or very near her armpits while she jumps.

Don't move on to the next level before your child is comfortable with the previous one.

FIRST LEVEL

Stand in waist- to chest-deep water and place your child in a sitting position on the pool wall, with your hands under her armpits. Count "1, 2, 3" and gently rub your hands under her armpits to cue her to jump, then move your hands 5–7.5cm (2–3in) under the water. When she jumps, catch her under her armpits as she submerges. Walk two steps backwards, gently guiding her with you for a brief swim, then lift her back to the surface. Over the weeks, increase the number of seconds your child remains submerged to two then three seconds.

SECOND LEVEL

Once you have practised the first level for a few weeks, move on to the second level. This is similar to the first level, but this time your child will swim unaided. Ask her to jump from a sitting position on the pool wall, but instead of catching her immediately as she jumps, hold your hands close to your body under the water and take two steps backwards to encourage her to swim towards you. Then catch her and bring her to the surface.

THIRD LEVEL

Once your child is proficient at the second level, repeat the technique but hold a toy under the water for your child to retrieve. This simple gesture adds focus and an additional element of fun, and encourages a good, horizontal streamlined position under water, as she will aim her eyes and face downwards towards the toy rather than simply towards her parent.

TURNING AROUND UNDER WATER

Now that your child has increased his breath-holding abilities and comfort under water, he is ready to turn 180° under water. This ability to turn will become one of the lynchpins of the important Safety Sequence (see pp108–09), which involves turning around to face the wall, grabbing the wall and climbing out.

OBJECTIVES AND TIPS

To build on the foundation skills learned in the Time to Go exit ritual of "Ring-a-ring of Rosies" (see p69).

To execute an assisted 180° turn in a vertical position.

If you feel an older beginner is starting to turn, encourage this by guiding his turn.

FIRST LEVEL

Follow the sequence for the well-practised Time to Go exit ritual of "Ring-a-ring of Rosies" (see p69). At the "We all fall down" verse, lift your child up for a breath, submerge him, but instead of raising him to the surface immediately, allow him to remain under water holding his breath for a slow count of "1, 2". Then raise him up out of the water and praise him. Practise once per lesson.

SECOND LEVEL

Once you have practised the first level for several weeks, and your child comfortably holds his breath for two seconds, you can try turning him. Follow the first level, but once he is under water, use your hands to slowly turn him 180° — either clockwise or anticlockwise depending on which way he naturally turns — so that he ends up facing your stomach. Raise him up and exclaim "Peek A Boo!"

INTERMEDIATES: STAGE TWO
(MINIMUM AGE 19 MONTHS)

STAGE TWO LESSON PLAN

REQUIREMENTS FOR STAGE TWO

Minimum Age: Your child should be at least 19 months old.

Skill Level: Your child has successfully completed Beginners: Stages One and Two and Intermediates: Stage One, as well as the Adaptations for Three- to Four-year-old Beginners if she started learning to swim over the age of 36 months. She can propel herself comfortably with a steady kick, face submerged, holding her breath for up to seven seconds without taking in water.

By this stage your child will have a good level of endurance and both physical and mental coordination. Because she will be able to swim under water for up to seven seconds with a strong, steady and effective kick, you can now add the important Safety Sequence (see pp108–09) to her repertoire. Although no child should ever be considered "drownproof", learning and consistently practising safety skills can help your child to make her way back to the edge of – and then out of – the pool in the event of an accidental water entry.

The Safety Sequence is a technique for experienced swimmers. Include it in the lesson plan only once the following techniques have been mastered comfortably by your child: Intermediate Swim to the Wall (see p104), Jump, Swim and Turn Back to the Wall (see p105) and Unaided Turn Under Water (see pp106–07). To maintain your child's focus and energy, once you are ready to practise the Safety Sequence eliminate the above three drills from the lesson plan and concentrate on the Safety Sequence instead.

LESSON PLAN

WARM UP 3–5 minutes
Practise kicking and chasing a toy or kicking drills. *pp56; 72*

SONG BREAK 3–5 minutes
Sing "The Wheels on the Bus" or a bathtime song. *p39*

WARM-UP DIPS 1–2 minutes
Short, cued dips using the technique for First Held Underwater Swim. *pp64–65*

ACTIVITY CIRCUIT 10–12 minutes total *pp52–53*
Structure the circuit as shown below. Go round 3–5 times.

- a) **Water Pouring Station** *pp46–47*
- b) **Monkey Walk or Basketball** *pp77; 45*
- c) **Jump, Dip and Swim** *pp98–99*
- d) **Pick-a-ball Game** *p49*
  For the pass between parents use Rob's Tai Chi Pass with your child wearing fins 5 times max *pp92–93*

To begin with, practise the skills under 1 (below, left). Once your child has mastered these exercises, replace with 2 (below, right).

1. INTERMEDIATE SWIM TO THE WALL
2–3 minutes, 3 times max *p104*

JUMP OFF THE WALL
2–3 minutes
Jump, Swim and Turn Back to the Wall (first or second level depending on ability) 3 times max *p105*

VERTICAL SUBMERSIONS AND TURNS
3 minutes
Unaided Turn Under Water (first, second or third level depending on ability) 3 times max *pp106–07*

2. THE SAFETY SEQUENCE
2–4 minutes total

- a) **Unaided Turn Under Water** (fourth level) 3 times max *p107*
- b) **The Safety Sequence** (first, second, third or fourth level depending on ability) 2 times max *pp108–09*

BALANCE or RUN AND JUMP 3–5 minutes *pp68; 51*

TIME TO GO 1 minute *p69*
Unaided Turn Under Water 2 times max *p106–07*

INTERMEDIATE SWIM TO THE WALL

Your child's ever-increasing comfort and confidence, his expanding lung capacity and his lengthening strong swim all indicate he is ready to develop his swimming capabilities further. For this swim, he will be much more independent as you will not manoeuvre or push him, merely guide him towards the wall with your fingertips.

OBJECTIVES

To create an increasingly more independent swim towards the wall while maintaining contact.

To encourage a horizontal body position and a steady kick.

To build on the skills gained in the Guided Swim to the Wall (see pp96–97).

1 Place a toy on the pool wall. With your child in the Pass Hold (see p43), stand 1.8m (6ft) away from the wall. Cue your child to go under water and submerge him. As his face enters the water, slip your dominant hand (your right hand if you are right-handed) out from under his armpit, move it over his back, and place your fingertips at the base of his head at the neck.

2 Slip your non-dominant hand out from under his other armpit gently and rest it by your side. Walk forwards, guiding him slowly towards the wall with your dominant hand. Allow him to swim to the wall, grab it, raise his head out of the water and pick up the toy as a reward. Make sure that the time submerged does not exceed your child's current breath-holding ability.

JUMP, SWIM AND TURN BACK TO THE WALL

You can now channel your child's sturdy, reliable, cued jump with a submersion into a jump with a short swim out to you, and then a jump with a short swim, above-water turn and a swim back to the wall. This confident jump needs to be safe, so make sure that your child waits for your count before leaving the wall.

OBJECTIVES

To encourage a jump from the wall that includes the increased breath holding of a swim.

To teach your child to transfer from a vertical lean to a swim.

To link the different skills of a jump off the wall with a swim, followed by a swim back to the wall.

FIRST LEVEL

Sit your child on the pool wall. Stand in chest-deep water 90–180cm (3–6ft) away from the wall and face your child. Hold your hands out and instruct him to jump out to you after your count. Count "1, 2, 3" to cue the jump. Allow your child to swim out to you, then reward him with a toy.

SECOND LEVEL

Once your child is confident at the first level, you can combine the jump off the wall and swim with an immediate swim back to the wall. Follow as for the first level, but once your child swims to you, catch him, lift him briefly for a breath, turn him around 180° and let him swim back to the wall (see opposite).

UNAIDED TURN UNDER WATER

For this new skill, you and your child will link several sequences in a specific order. She can already submerge vertically holding her breath for several seconds, and you've helped her to turn 180° under water — now you are going to teach her to do this turn independently, first to you, then to the wall.

TEACHING TIPS

Keep your hands close to your child while she is learning these skills. You may need to help to turn her or lift her for air.

Note which side your child turns towards naturally — which shoulder is she looking over? Help her turn in this direction if necessary.

FIRST LEVEL

Play "Peek A Boo". Stand in waist- to chest-deep water facing your partner, 60cm (2ft) apart. Hold your child vertically facing towards you, so the receiver is hidden from your child's view. The receiver should call out "Where am I?" Your child should turn her chin over one shoulder to look for the receiver, thus initiating a body rotation. If she does not twist round, turn her 180° to face the receiver. Exclaim, "Peek A Boo!" Repeat several times per lesson for at least two lessons.

SECOND LEVEL

Once your child is confident at the first level, you can move on to the second. Stand holding your child as for the first level, but this time the receiver places a dive ring between her thumb and index finger. Turn your child towards the receiver, who should show her the ring, placing it under water in line with her stomach, then turn your child back round to face you. Tell her to "Get the ring!" Give her a cue to go under water, submerge her and release her. She should turn, grab the ring and then be lifted by the receiver.

THIRD LEVEL

Once your child turns every time at the second level, you can move on to the third. Hide a toy on the pool wall. Stand with your child facing you 25–30cm (10–12in) from the wall. Turn her so she can see the ring, then turn her back to face you and ask her to find the ring then grab the wall. Staying above water, she should look over her shoulder, rotating her body and grab the wall. Practise two to three times per lesson.

FOURTH LEVEL

Once your child accomplishes the third level successfully, you can move on to the fourth. Stand as for the third level, then give her the cue to go under water, submerge her and gently release her. She should turn under water to grab the wall and find the toy. Practise two to three times per lesson for several weeks.

THE SAFETY SEQUENCE

This vital safety sequence should be used in addition to the safety plan on pp24–25. It will teach your child to jump off the wall safely, turn around by herself in the water, swim back to the wall, grab the wall and exit the pool. This means that if your child ever faces an accidental water entry, this sequence will enable her to swim confidently and safely to the wall and climb out of the pool.

OBJECTIVES

To link multiple skills together in sequence to ensure water safety.

To rehearse water entry by simulating a fall into water in a non-threatening fashion.

To encourage a repeatable, rehearsable sequence that is implemented automatically in the event of an accidental water entry.

FIRST LEVEL

1 Sit your child on the pool wall. Tell her that her job is to jump in, turn around under water and come back to the wall (you can put a toy on the wall to encourage her). Place your hip firmly against the wall on the side towards which your child usually turns (see pp100–01). Place your hand that is nearest to her under her armpit and stretch out your other arm so your hand is about 90–120cm (3–4ft) from the wall. With this hand, splash the water as a marker of how far you want her to jump. Cue the jump by counting "1, 2, 3", then keep your nearest hand under her armpit lightly so you can shadow her jump and make sure she leaves the wall correctly.

2 Once she has jumped, raise the elbow of your extended arm and use your fingertips to scoop and turn her around at the base of the head, guiding her back to the wall. Your other hand should now splash near the wall, creating a visible and audible target. Once she has reached the wall, boost one of her knees up and help her to climb out.

SECOND LEVEL

Once your child can perform this sequence with less guidance, practise without shadowing her or guiding her back to the wall, but continue to splash near the wall to create a target. Help her out of the pool.

THIRD LEVEL

Once your child is competent at the second level and has practised for several weeks, ask your partner to sit next to your child on the pool edge with their toes in the water. Tell your child to "Jump in, turn around, look for [your partner's] toes, grab the wall and climb out and sit next to her". Follow the sequence for the second level, but do not splash the water near the wall as your child should aim for your partner's toes. At the end, your child should climb out and sit next to your partner.

FOURTH LEVEL

Once your child has competently practised the third level for a number of weeks, you can progress to the fourth level. Use the same technique as for the third level, but for this level your partner should sit in a chair on the deck. This time, after performing the sequence under your watchful eye while you are in the water, your child should climb out of the pool to hug your partner, thus taking him far away from the pool's edge.

INTERMEDIATES: STAGE THREE
(MINIMUM AGE THREE YEARS)

STAGE THREE LESSON PLAN

Children in this age group are great characters with boundless energy and vivid imaginations. They love to chat, sing and play games, and also like to work for rewards – motivation and encouragement are key to their learning. They will progress well when learning in a group environment because they love mimicking their peers and demonstrating their skills to their friends.

You will find that by now your child is a good swimmer, can link together skills in a sequence and her coordination has improved greatly due to her physical development. As she can now kick well and spend a significant amount of time under water, she can progress to more complicated skills such as floating.

Skills such as Coming Up for Air (see pp112–13) and Back Floating (see p117) take time and patience to master. Never force breathing or floating skills and introduce back floating gradually, depending on your child's ever-increasing levels of relaxation, trust and readiness. It may take months to accomplish these skills, but once acquired, they offer your child increased mobility and safety in the water.

LESSON PLAN

COMING UP FOR AIR – ASSISTED

Once a child learns to come up for a breath, he will be able to swim for longer, resurfacing again and again as he explores the pool. Surfacing for a breath takes several months to achieve fully, but with time and practice, and by instructing your child in the correct technique, he will gain a new freedom in the water.

TEACHING TIPS

Starting this skill at too young an age results in your child swimming vertically in the water, which is frustrating for him and exhausting.

Supporting your child at the waist or hips creates a fulcrum that prompts him to move his arms and hands forwards and raise his head.

FIRST LEVEL

Stand in chest-deep water, with your partner 4.5m (15ft) ahead of you. Hold your child in the Pass Hold (see p43) and cue him to go under water. As his face enters the water release him and walk along beside him. At the end of his usual breath holding (by now up to 10 seconds), slip your hands under his armpits and lift him up for a breath. Facing your child, the receiver should take an audible gulp of air and then close his mouth while you say "take a breath". Listen to check that your child has taken a breath, then continue to swim him under water to the receiver, who should pick him up and praise him. Practise for at least six lessons.

SECOND LEVEL

Once your child takes a breath every time you lift him in the first level, let him try to lift his own head out of the water. Follow the first level, but at his usual breath-taking point, place your hands at his waist. Your child can lean his torso onto your hands to give him leverage, paddle his hands, arch his back, lift his chin up out of the water and take a breath. He can then submerge his head again and continue his swim. Initially you may need to tilt your wrists upwards to help him come up for a breath. Practise for at least six lessons.

THIRD LEVEL

Once your child is competent at the second level, move your hands down from his waist to his hips. This alters the amount of leverage he has, making him push harder on the water with his hands to raise his head for air. Practise for at least six lessons.

FOURTH LEVEL

Once your child is confident at the third level, move your hands to your child's thighs so that you are providing even less leverage and he needs to push even harder to come up for air. Practise for at least the next six lessons.

COMING UP FOR AIR – EQUIPMENT

Mastering the skill of surfacing for air takes months of practice, but if you wish, you can use equipment and toys to improve technique and body position and motivate your child. Hoops and noodles provide a focus, while fins and barbells allow your child to experience a new skill before he perfects it.

TEACHING TIPS

If you are practising alone, you can adapt the third option by using the wall to support one end of the noodle. If you are in a group, you can make things easier by holding equipment for each other.

Prompt your child with the phrase: "Take a breath, eyes in, big kicks!"

FIRST OPTION

Stand facing your child in waist-deep water, with a barbell between you. Ask your child to hold the barbell with both hands and straight arms. Tell him to take a breath, then gently place his face in the water. Walk backwards as your child swims the barbell towards you. Tap the crown of his head and take a deep breath to encourage him to mimic you and breathe in, then tell him, "put your eyes in and splash with your feet". At the start, you may need to tow the barbell or add fins for greater propulsion and to assist with the head lift.

SECOND OPTION

Stand in waist- to chest-deep water opposite your
partner, 3–3.6m (10–12ft) apart. Your partner should have
a puppet. Tell your child "when the puppet is up, you are
up; when it is down, you are down". With your child in
the Pass Hold (see p43) cue him to go under water and,
as your partner places the puppet under water, swim your
child to your partner. Follow your child, and after a few
seconds your partner should raise the puppet out of the
water and your child should lift his head. Repeat until
your child reaches your partner.

THIRD OPTION

Make a bridge by holding two noodles on top of the
water, so they are 1.5–1.8m (5–6ft) apart. (Or make a
hoop tunnel with two hoops partially submerged held
1.5–1.8m (5–6ft) apart.) Instruct your child to swim
under the first bridge, come up to take a breath in the
middle, then go under the second bridge. Initially, your
partner may need to help him to come up by using the
different leverage supports shown on pages 112–13.

FRONT AND BACK FLOATING

Floating, which should be done with free will, not imposed, requires experience and trust. We introduce floating to our most experienced swimmers who are totally relaxed and in harmony with the aquatic environment, rather than to younger, less competent swimmers who may be alarmed by these new positions.

TEACHING TIPS

Let your child hold a toy, recite the alphabet or count to occupy and relax her while she is floating.

Technique is not as important as the fact your child is relaxed.

By watching someone else float – a parent, sibling or peer – your child is more likely to try this skill.

FLOATING ON THE FRONT

1 While you hold your child, ask your partner to demonstrate a front float. Point out to your child how the knees are bent, the arms are held out with the elbows bent, the head is looking down and the body is relaxed and not wriggling.

2 Stand in the Face-to-face Hold (see p43) and tell your child that it is now her turn to front float and that you will help her. Ask her to "take a big breath and put your eyes in". You can initiate this by taking a breath audibly and visibly. Gently release your hands from under her armpits and dangle them under her as she floats and holds your outstretched arms.

FLOATING ON THE BACK

1 As with floating on the front, show your child how your partner floats on his back and point out what each part of his body is doing. Alternatively, lie your child on his back on a large foam mat and point out what all his body parts are doing when floating.

2 Tell your child it is her turn (or time to try it in the water if she has been floating on the mat), and hold her facing away from you, with the sun behind you so there is no glare. Place her cheek next to yours and touch your palm lightly to her other cheek. Rest her head on your shoulder while she leans back from a vertical position. Slowly lower your shoulder to the water so the back of her head touches the water. (This way she won't feel like she is falling.) Place your free hand in the small of her back for support. Point out how key body parts should be positioned: "look back at me, head back, chin to the sky, tummy up, palms up catching sun, arms and legs relaxed, no wriggling." Practise two to three times per lesson.

SWIMMING ON THE BACK

Being able to swim on his back means that your child will always be able to breathe – a very important safety skill. Children who are relaxed and ready for this new skill find this novel position, with their mouth and eyes out of the water, a fun new way to move in the pool, so expect lots of giggling.

OBJECTIVES

To instil the correct body alignment for later back swimming.

To refine the kick movement – it becomes more hip-generated in this position, with straighter legs and the feet just below the surface.

To establish the foundation for backstroke and freestyle drills.

FIRST LEVEL

Play a game of "Tugboat and *QEII*", where your child is the tugboat and you the liner. Stand behind your child and position him on his back, holding a barbell at his waist so he can hold it and touch it to his belly button. His head should touch your chest. Instruct your child to push you with his head, saying "be a strong tugboat and push me into port". Walk backwards slowly as he kicks and maintains contact with your chest, pushing against you. Tell him to look you in the eyes as he kicks, giving him frequent prompts: "head back, tummy up, push me, little kicks". Praise him for being a strong tugboat.

SECOND LEVEL

1 Once your child is happy playing "Tugboat", try playing the game of "Food Delivery". Stand 90–120cm (3–4ft) opposite your partner. Ask your child to name her favourite snack, then position her so she is floating on her back and place the imaginary snack on her stomach. Tell her, "deliver the snack [to the receiver], but keep your tummy up so it doesn't become soggy".

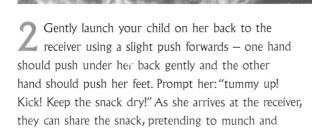

2 Gently launch your child on her back to the receiver using a slight push forwards – one hand should push under her back gently and the other hand should push her feet. Prompt her: "tummy up! Kick! Keep the snack dry!" As she arrives at the receiver, they can share the snack, pretending to munch and enjoy it. For variety, you can also have your child push off the wall with her feet and glide gently on her back towards you with her tummy up. She can then share the imaginary snack with you.

180° ROLL DURING A SWIM

Changing orientation during a swim creates a new way to take a breath. For an experienced back swimmer, this is another important safety skill. To make this technique fun for your child to learn, pretend he is a hot dog, pouring imaginary mustard and ketchup all over him, then saying "hot dog!" when you want your child to roll and wash it all off.

OBJECTIVES AND TIPS

To teach a 180° rolling technique from prone to supine and supine to prone.

To encourage taking a breath before rolling into the water.

To associate a command ("hot dog!") with the action of rolling.

If your child is on your left-hand side, simply reverse the directions.

FIRST LEVEL

1 Tell your child, "we're going to roll you over and put ketchup and mustard on you like a hot dog". Standing in chest-deep water, 2.4m (8ft) opposite your partner, place your child in the Pass Hold (see p43) on your right-hand side. Cue him to go under water and, as he swims, walk along with him, keeping your hands on him. When he almost reaches the receiver say, "hot dog!" and roll him towards you with your right hand, pushing him away from you gently with your left hand. He will roll 180°, bringing his face to the surface.

2 Now that he is on his back, you and the receiver should "squirt" your child with the imaginary sauces, then tell him that you're going to wash it all off. Hold your child on his back on your right-hand side with your left arm under his back and your left hand holding his far armpit. Your right hand should hold him under his nearest armpit. Begin a held swim and then say, "hot dog!" To turn him, pull your left hand towards you and push your right hand away from you, rolling your child so his face is in the water, then rolling him back up again after a few seconds.

SECOND LEVEL

1 Once your child is confident with the assisted rolls in the first level, you can let him try rolling himself. Stand in chest-deep water opposite your partner, 2.4m (8ft) apart, holding your child so that he is floating on his back. Gently launch your child to the receiver using a slight push forwards. Just before he reaches the receiver say, "hot dog!" This should cue him to roll over into a prone position on his front and finish swimming to the receiver.

2 Repeat step one, but with your child swimming on his front. Cue your child to go under water and launch him for an unaided swim. Just before he reaches the receiver say, "hot dog!", which should cue him to roll onto his back.

Once your child is confident performing unaided single rolls, he can start doing a roll-and-return cycle, first rolling one way from his front to his back, then taking a breath and rolling back the same way onto his front before reaching the receiver.

DIVING FOR RINGS

One of the most thrilling rites of passage for a young swimmer is gaining the ability to perform a surface dive and retrieve a ring or toy off the bottom of the pool. Not only does this skill promote the ability to navigate under water – thus increasing comfort and safety in the water – it also fosters self-esteem.

FIRST LEVEL

1 Tell your child to "kick hard" to the bottom, grab the ring and "kick hard" to come up. Drop a dive ring at a depth of 90–105cm (3–3½ft), then stand back at a diagonal angle to it. Holding your child in the Pass Hold (see p43), cue her to go under water. Submerge her by giving her a slight push diagonally and down, then release her.

2 Your child should swim down towards the pool floor, grab the ring when it is within her reach, push off the pool floor and look upwards towards the surface, angling her body for the ascent. She will return upwards either by floating up or by kicking. She may try both tactics and then develop a preference for using one of them.

3 As your child returns to the surface, catch her and praise her for a job well done. Practise this sequence several times per lesson.

SECOND LEVEL

Once your child is confident at the first level, withdraw your assistance gradually by decreasing the strength of your push and encouraging your child to "put your head down and kick", initiating a jackknife or pike position. She may eventually propel herself using both arms to bring her down. You can also sink multiple rings to lengthen the time spent manoeuvring under water and hence increase her lung capacity.

RESOURCES

ORGANIZATIONS

British Red Cross
One of the leading providers of first aid training.
www.redcross.org

British Swimming
National governing body for swimming and diving.
Its members are the Amateur Swimming Association
(England), Scottish Amateur Swimming Association
and Welsh Amateur Swimming Association.
www.britishswimming.org

Lifestyle Swim School
Founded by Rob and Kathy McKay, organizes
teacher training, workshops and referrals.
Creators and suppliers of "Diaper Dolphins"
video series for parents.
www.babyswimming.com
email: babyswimschool@aol.com

Royal Life Saving Society Australia
A leading provider of water safety, swimming
and lifesaving education.
www.royallifesaving.com.au

Swim Australia
Teaches water safety and swimming.
www.swimaustralia.org.au

World Aquatic Babies Congress
Founded by Virginia Hunt Newman, focuses on aquatic
programmes for babies, toddlers and young children.
www.waterbabies.org
email: WABC@waterbabies.org

SUPPLIERS OF EQUIPMENT, CLOTHES AND TOYS

For fins (flippers), goggles, noodles, swimming and UV suits, water toys and other equipment, try the following websites:

Aqua Shop
www.aquashop.com.au

Baby Swim Store
www.babyswimstore.com

Bambino Mio
www.bambinomio.co.uk

Kiefer Swim Shop
www.kiefer.com
email: esales@kiefer.com

Pooltoy.com
www.pooltoy.com
email: info@pooltoy.com

Sprint Aquatics
www.sprintaquatics.com
email: info@sprintaquatics.com

Swimrite
www.swimrite.com

The Great Little Trading Company
www.gltc.co.uk

The-Swim-Store.com
www.the-swim-store.com

INDEX

ACKNOWLEDGMENTS

AUTHORS' ACKNOWLEDGMENTS

Our heartfelt thanks go to: our parents, John and Bobbie McKay and Bill and Irene Kement for always loving us, supporting our efforts and setting an outstanding example of good parenting; our brothers, Scott McKay and Michael Kement for sharing with us happy, active and playful childhoods and lasting bonds of friendship; our daughters, Heather and Brianne McKay who taught us firsthand the joys of being a parent, continue to enrich our lives with their beautiful spirits and who encouraged us to write this book.

Our sincere thanks go to the "mother" of infant swimming, Virginia Hunt Newman, a pioneering advocate of the gentle, positive approach to teaching babies to swim, for her friendship, inspiration, insight, ethics and vision; Chuck Gaspari, our friend and attorney, whose counsel, motivation and foresight helped us throughout the writing, publishing and marketing process; the entire DK team whose dedicated efforts and skill brought this book into being; Steve Graves, founder of the National Swim School Association and executive director of the World Aquatic Baby Congress for his vast knowledge of swimming, his always wise and insightful comments, for his support and enthusiasm over the years; longtime friends John Spannuth, founder of the United States Water Fitness Association, Buck Dawson, founding director of the International Swimming Hall of Fame and Bob Duenkel, curator of the ISHOF, for their steadfast encouragement; Florida Atlantic University for the use of their pool during our photo shoot; Art and Irena Scroggie for the use of their home pool during our photo shoot; Vinnie Gordon of Gordon Homes for her help in scouting locations; Lauren Glaun of Sunstoppers for so promptly coming to our rescue with beautiful UV suits for the photo shoot.

Finally, our thanks go to the thousands of parents and babies we have had the privilege to teach over the years who have enriched our lives and our life's work; the babies and the parents featured in this book for helping to convey to the world the boundless joy and freedom of movement experienced when learning to swim with a gentle, child-paced approach.

AUTHORS' BIOGRAPHY

Rob and Kathy McKay have been practising their child-centred approach to teaching young children to swim for over 23 years. Their Lifestyle Swim School in Florida has international acclaim, and they have trained teachers from around the world in how to use their innovative methods. Rob serves on the board of the World Aquatic Baby Congress, and has won numerous awards for his contribution to baby swimming.

PUBLISHER'S ACKNOWLEDGMENTS

Dorling Kindersley would like to thank all the families who gave their time to model for this book: Eddie and Lauren Ames with David and AJ; Melissa Babey with Brandon and Hunter; Melissa Biggs with Tiffany; Scott Bradley with Skyann; Mickey and Nati Charney; Manu and Lisa Chauhan with Kai; Robin DeStefano with Jenna; Colette Duenkel with Teagan; Esther Fix with Benjamin; Kristen Gaspari with Jonas and James; Cindy Giaquinto with Jenna; Fran Janicki with Ethan; Karen Kahane with Brianna; Keith and Stacey Kern with Elisabeth; Leimomi Lane with Kaui; Gillian Lopez with Fox; Heather McKay; Victoria Neil with Tyler; Luis and JB Perdomo with Sofia; Cherly Price with Danny; Candace Pritchard with Carson; Hervé and Sylvia Rivere with Lily; Becky Schmidt with Slade; Irena Scroggie with Nicole and Sophia; Karen and Jim Shields with Joshua; Danté Sigona; Joshua and Kinga Snowhorn with Alma and Luca; Regina and Charles Stabile with Adrianna; Terri Stetz with Jacklyn Lipp; Stephanie Welch with Gavin.

Dorling Kindersley would also like to thank photographer Zena Holloway, her assistant Vanessa Sherry, and make-up artist Kim Allegra; the Great Little Trading Company for the loan of props; Florida Atlantic University and Art and Irena Scroggie for the use of their pools; Lavish Locations; Jacquie Meredith (proofreader); Hilary Bird (indexer); Adam Powley (jacket copywriter); Carrie Love (jacket editor); and Tony Chung (jacket designer).

Picture credit
p38, Getty Images / PT Santana.